Praise for *W*

"Anyone attempting to enter the workforce and deal with The Man without this funny, seditious, and crucial document should have his cubicle examined."

—**Stanley Bing, *Fortune* magazine columnist and bestselling author of *Crazy Bosses***

"I found Jeffrey's book ridonkulously amusing. I was a secretary for five years and feel like I know each of the anecdotal characters personally. Needless to say the suggestion on how to celebrate secretary's day hit especially close to home." —**Jennifer Perkins, proprietress of Naughty Secretary Club and Host of Craft Lab**

"At last, a veritable how-to on self-preservation, entertainment, and vengeance in the workplace. Jeffrey Yamaguchi guides readers through the slippery terrains of the corporate maze with expertise that only comes from years of wriggling under The Man's oppressive thumb. He exposes the truths of corporate life with humor and a razor-sharp wit. Whether you are a rookie or veteran cubicle dweller, *Working for the Man* will make you proud to work in cubicle land." —**Kim Waldauer, CubeNews1.com**

"This book should be handed out to every disgruntled office drone in America. It's guaranteed to inject humor and creativity into even the most soul-suckingly dull workplace."

—**Lilit Marcus, cofounder of www.savetheassistants.com**

"Ferocious, hilarious, and rebellious, *Working for the Man* is both an entertaining guide to the hell of cubicle land—and a map out of it. Yamaguchi skewers bosses, coworkers, and corporate America in this comprehensive manual to staying sane and wreaking havoc in the workplace, and he does it with a facile 'been there, done that, got fired' attitude."

—**Bill Keaggy, author of *Milk Eggs Vodka: Grocery Lists Lost and Found***

continued . . .

Praise for *52 Projects*

"The projects in this book will help you expand your imagination and also help you take stock of your life. Perfect for those times when you have a serious creative block. The variety of projects are presented in a way to allow you to find your artistic side, your creative voice, or explore yourself or your friends."
— **Craftzine.com**

"This is the kind of book that is hard to write about because it's more like an event than a book. Or a way to look at life a bit differently. It's big (like *big ideas*, big) and it's one of those books where, even if you read just a few pages, you will remember what you read for a long time." — **Angry Chicken**

"There's something about the thrill of creativity—seeing something through from idea to execution. The feeling of purpose that comes from having a project to work on, that you've got something worthwhile to spend your time and energy on, beyond the normal nine-to-five and day-to-day routine. In that vein, Jeffrey Yamaguchi's *52 Projects* is packed with enough ideas and inspiration to last a long, long time." — **AbsoluteWrite.com**

"The projects contained in this book are for crafters, scrapbookers, photographers, artists, or mothers, fathers, aunts, uncles, or businesspeople. All you need as required tools are a camera, paper and pen, and imagination. How you interpret them is up to you . . ." — **Scrapability**

"The book is a perfect antidote to creative blocks of all stripes. If you're feeling *verklemmt*, pick up the book, or pop on over to the 52 Projects website, and crib some inspirado . . . *52 Projects* will help you build up those atrophied creative muscles . . . or if they're in pretty good shape already, keep you sleek, supple, and toned." — **ExtremeCraft.com**

"[*52 Projects*] provides inspiration to move around within your creative reality and explore different realms of who you are as a crafter or artisan. Within its pages are the tools to integrate your creativity and originality into all elements of your life, be it family, friendship, or work. You'll love it!"
— **Creative Techniques**

Working for the Man

INSPIRING
AND
SUBVERSIVE
PROJECTS
FOR
RESIDENTS
OF
CUBICLE
LAND

Jeffrey Yamaguchi

ILLUSTRATIONS BY
Danny Jock

A
PERIGEE
BOOK

A PERIGEE BOOK
Published by the Penguin Group
Penguin Group (USA) Inc.
375 Hudson Street, New York, New York 10014, USA

Penguin Group (Canada), 90 Eglinton Avenue East, Suite 700, Toronto, Ontario M4P 2Y3, Canada
(a division of Pearson Penguin Canada Inc.)
Penguin Books Ltd., 80 Strand, London WC2R 0RL, England
Penguin Group Ireland, 25 St. Stephen's Green, Dublin 2, Ireland (a division of Penguin Books Ltd.)
Penguin Group (Australia), 250 Camberwell Road, Camberwell, Victoria 3124, Australia
(a division of Pearson Australia Group Pty. Ltd.)
Penguin Books India Pvt. Ltd., 11 Community Centre, Panchsheel Park, New Delhi—110 017, India
Penguin Group (NZ), 67 Apollo Drive, Rosedale, North Shore 0632, New Zealand
(a division of Pearson New Zealand Ltd.)
Penguin Books (South Africa) (Pty.) Ltd., 24 Sturdee Avenue, Rosebank, Johannesburg 2196,
South Africa

Penguin Books Ltd., Registered Offices: 80 Strand, London WC2R 0RL, England

While the author has made every effort to provide accurate telephone numbers and Internet addresses at the time of publication, neither the publisher nor the author assumes any responsibility for errors, or for changes that occur after publication. Further, the publisher does not have
any control over and does not assume any responsibility for author or third-party websites or
their content.

Copyright © 2007 by Jeffrey Yamaguchi
Illustrations by Danny Jock
Cover art by Getty Images
Cover design by Ben Gibson
Text design by Stephanie Huntwork

First edition: November 2007

Library of Congress Cataloging-in-Publication Data

Yamaguchi, Jeffrey.
   Working for the man : inspiring and subversive projects for residents of cubicle land /
Jeffrey Yamaguchi— 1st ed.
      p.   cm.
   ISBN-13: 978-0-399-53371-6
   1. Work—Humor.   2. Offices—Humor.   I. Title.
   PN6231.W644Y36   2007
   818'.607—dc22   2007025868

PRINTED IN THE UNITED STATES OF AMERICA

10   9   8   7   6   5   4   3   2   1

For my sister Jodie

"I will work harder."

—Boxer, in George Orwell's *Animal Farm*

ACKNOWLEDGMENTS

Thanks to readers of and contributors to my websites, www.workingfortheman.com and www.52projects.com. I've been working on those sites in different ways for years now, and all your letters and mentions and contributions have been deeply meaningful and truly inspirational to me.

Thanks to Kevin Sampsell, Liz at Quimby's, Rachel at Atomic Books, Kath Red at www.whipup.net, the one-of-a-kind Larry Smith of www.smithmag.net, SuperNaturale Tsia Carson, Andrea / Hula Seventy, Diane Gilleland, Kelly Love Johnson, Jason Boog of www.thepublishingspot.com, Rudy DeDominicis (Mr. Ridonkulous himself), Michelle Howry, Ada Chu, Justin Nisbet, Matt Thomas, and Gordon Hurd.

Thanks also to the insightful and supportive Meg Leder, who truly helped me shape this project and who was sort of The Man on this book, but in a good way. Thanks to designer Ben Gibson for sticking it to the man (not Meg) with his spot-on cover. Thanks to Danny Jock for doing his Danny-Jockian ("not too caveman") magic on the illustrations. Thanks to Faith Hamlin, who makes sure all this gets to happen; to Courtney Miller-Callihan; and to John Duff and Jennifer Eck as well.

Thanks to my family, of course, the most important people in my life—my mother and father, my brother Scott, and my sister Jodie (my #1 fan / strongest person I know). And thanks to my one and only Juhu for still at least half-listening (or as she puts it, "multitasking") to all my negative ramblings and oft-repeated diatribes complaining that this world (especially the world of work) is just not making me happy, then kicking my ass for being such a pathetic piece of nothing.

DISCLAIMER

oing some of the things in this book may get you fired. You've been warned.

Advice regarding this disclaimer:
Just don't get caught.

Note on the advice regarding the disclaimer:
If you do get caught, you have only yourself to blame.

CONTENTS

'm going to keep this short and simple.*

If this were a work project, there'd be someone forcing you to do it, there would be many voices giving contradictory direction, and you'd have to spend a great deal of time updating your boss and then contending with his insults/ideas. Throughout the process, there would be many people telling you they want to hear what you have to say, only to not listen to a word you say, and there would be endless meetings, at which people would either ask really stupid questions or berate your lack of progress on the project, or both. You would probably have to stay late night after night and practically kill yourself to get the project done, and possibly miss your deadline, at which point you would be screamed at and scolded like a child, most likely in front of lots of people. At the very end, you'd have to do some kind of report involving a Power-Point presentation and a lot of spreadsheets that people would be harassing you to finish. Of course, once you actually sent out the report, no one would bother to read it. If the project was a success, your boss would take full credit. If it was a failure, you would take the sole blame, even though

---

*I used that opening sentence with the full knowledge that those words often precede the longest, most dreadful meetings at work.

> **WORKING FOR THE MAN**
> **RULE #1** • We are all
> working for the man.

there were most likely extenuating circumstances (like your boss) that actually made the project fail.

That's all just a part of working for the man. But in *Working for the Man*—the book—that's not the case at all. Indeed, the book rails against all of the above and reveals ways to get out from underneath such nonsense.

Working for the Man is about taking back and taking hold of your experience at work. This book contains a series of insights about the workplace and offers up a whole host of projects and ideas (not "action items") on how to subvert your workaday frustration and truly enrich the time you have to spend on the clock. There may be no escape, but that does not mean you have serve out your mandatory sentence in a disgruntled state that gets worse as the years wear on—you can and should have a fun and fulfilling experience at work—the place where you spend more of your waking hours than anywhere else.

The ideas and projects run the gamut—from the resourceful to the surreptitious. Some may lead to promotions, others may get you fired (if you are caught, that is). There are those you may feel cross the line and a few that are so stupid you might believe that they were written by a Human Resources plant. The overall emphasis here is to encourage you to tap your creativity, gregariousness, and competitive nature, and reclaim what might seem like wasted hours in the workplace to create not just a better professional life, but a better life in general.

Naturally, in the spirit of dictating your own terms, the information in this book is yours for the taking, to do with it as you wish. No meetings, no spreadsheets. No progress reports. No supervision.

You are the boss. Proceed as you see fit.

**WORKING FOR THE MAN
RULE #2** · There are some people who think, *Hey, I am the man!* Sorry, idiot, you are also working for the man. Unfortunately for you, because of what you were just thinking, and maybe even saying out loud, you are also a jackass. That, and people probably don't like you very much.

he destroyer of your good moods. The obliterator of your peace of mind. The frayer of your nerves. The ignitor of your ire. The raiser of your stress. This is none other than, let the echoing clamor of boos begin, your boss.

You'll always have a boss. Even if you run your own company, you still have a boss, in the form of a major client or investor. There's always someone who can call you up at an inopportune time and make crazy, unreasonable demands in a very rude, high-decibel manner.

WORKING FOR THE MAN
RULE #3 • When your boss is telling you about a new assignment and keeps repeating "This is only for a few weeks," bear down for a long haul—six months to a year (at the minimum).

And because that's just the way it is, now and for the rest of your working life, your best and only option is to figure out ways to deal with all the bad bosses you'll have over the years and all the crap that they'll throw at you. It's a project, all right. Mark it high priority. Make it an urgent matter. Get to work ASAP. Yes, you may have to work on it over the weekend. The good news is that, though this work is being done with your boss in mind, it is not *for* your boss. It is for you.

to-do list

ASSESS YOUR BOSS

Have you ever been called into your boss's office, unscheduled, and found someone from HR sitting right next to her, both of them with a piece of paper in front of them—a prepared list of all the things you've failed to do or didn't do right?

That is a meeting held to tell you three things:

1. They want to fire you, but to protect themselves and make your termination aboveboard legally, they need to follow an established process and have on the record that they gave you an official warning and explained in detail why they think you are unfit for the job.

2. They're hoping you'll just quit.
3. The next time you are called into this office, you will be fired.

It's a very humiliating experience. You are totally unprepared and stuttering—all your excuses making you actually sound as bad as they are saying you are—and they are working off a prepared list of your offenses and essentially denouncing your efforts on the job, based on rehearsed talking points.

So why not assume that this meeting will be called at some point? And how amazing would it be to have your own prepared checklist and rehearsed talking points against your boss.

It's simple to compile this information—either keep a file, create a spreadsheet on your computer, or use a separate notebook—whatever is easiest to quickly update each time your boss makes some kind of infraction. The Boss Evaluation Sheet on the following page will provide guidance in making sure your records cover all aspects of your boss's job performance.

For example, if she's late, make a note. If she misses a meeting, make a note. If she misses deadlines, make a note. If she leaves early, make a note. And be sure to print out and make copies of her rude, angry, disparaging, or nonsensical emails.

This way, when you get called in for that meeting, you can

> **WORKING FOR THE MAN RULE #4** • If your boss keeps repeating the phrase "This is just for a little while," it's safe to assume that this "temporary" assignment will be a part of your workload permanently.

**WORKING FOR THE MAN
RULE #5 •** If you ever find out that your boss had a nose job, you won't be able to stop yourself from referring to her as "Nosejob" whenever you talk about her behind her back.

say, "Let me just grab some notes." You may not be fully prepared to exonerate yourself from all the infractions they've documented on you—it's a kangaroo court anyway—but at least you can bring your boss down with you.

"Well I really appreciate this honest feedback," you can say. "I'm a little surprised to be hearing this from my direct supervisor—it's actually quite inappropriate since she actually has a record—which I've been documenting—with very similar issues and infractions."

Certainly you'll get cut off. You'll be told that this isn't about your boss, that the point of this meeting is *you*. But your point will be made. It will be made loud and clear. Make sure to leave the documentation with the HR person. Mention that you have copies.

Of course, items 1, 2, and 3 still hold, even more so after your little uppity evidence display. Start looking for a new job, pronto.

boss evaluation sheet

Rate your boss on the following items on a scale of 1 to 5, where

1 = Unacceptable, fails to meet expectations
2 = Weak effort, in need of improvement

3 = Satisfactory
4 = Strong effort, good work
5 = Excellence

COMMUNICATION SKILLS

Runs meetings: (How pointless does your boss make the meetings he/she runs?)_____.

Verbal communication: (How rude is your boss when speaking to you?)_____

_____

WORKING FOR THE MAN
RULE #6 • The boss who says, "I want it to look cool!" in describing what he wants is usually the uncoolest person in the office, and wouldn't know cool if it hit him right in the head.

Written communication: (How little sense does your boss make via email?)_____

_____

Provides direction: (How does your boss assign and approve work despite a total lack of direction?)_____

_____

Cleary states goals: (How does your boss manage without any clear goals?)_____

WORK QUALITY

On time / attendance: (How good are your boss's excuses for showing up late, and is he/she actually available when "working from home"?)_____

Attention to detail: (How much unnecessary nitpicking goes on when your boss is evaluating your work/presentations?)

_____

Produced work: (Does your boss take all the credit for your work?)_____

INNOVATION
New ideas: (How does your boss implement ideas taken from items read in magazines/newspapers/books?) _____

_____

Handles roadblocks: (How does your boss throw blame around when things are going badly on a project?) _____

_____

Adapts to new information and changing conditions: (How much time does your boss waste trying to overcome problems that he/she was alerted to but didn't heed months before?)_____

INTERPERSONAL SKILLS
Listens: (Does your boss ever actually hear what you are saying?)_____

_____

WORKING FOR THE MAN
RULE #7 • If the project you are heading up is a success, your boss will take credit for it.

Manages crises: (How quickly does your boss figure out who to blame for failure?)_____

Treats staff with respect: (How does your boss get away with treating people so poorly?)_____
_____

WORKING FOR THE MAN
RULE #8 • If your project is not a success, your boss will make sure that you, and you alone, are blamed for its failure.

EMPLOYEE MANAGEMENT

Communicates goals: (How does your boss actually get you to work hard on ill-conceived projects that are based on his/her terrible ideas?) _____

Encourages success: (Does your boss know when to stop yelling?)_____

Offers opportunities for new challenges and promotions: (How does your boss spin the reason he/she can't promote you?)_____

PLEASE DESCRIBE THE FOLLOWING WITH REGARD TO YOUR BOSS. BE AS SPECIFIC AS POSSIBLE

Strengths: (Do you have anything nice to say about your boss at all?)_____

Weaknesses: (Challenge yourself by writing your boss's weaknesses in less than a page.)_____

Areas for improvement: (Will you be able to continue to work for your boss even though he/she will most certainly get worse than he/she already is?)_____

THE REVERSE SLAM

So you have a boss that knows exactly how to make you feel like you're never going to get it all done. He's dashing off one-sentence emails, one after the other. Faster than you can read and process one, six more have piled up in your inbox. And even when he's out of the office, he's calling you up with this request and that emergency. How does he do this? Very simple—that's all he's doing: calling you up and sending you things to do and making absurd requests for information, and then responding to the work that you turn in as you try to keep up with the ever-expanding workload. This is nothing more than a technique. Your boss thinks he's working hard because he's "delegating," but really, he's just jerking through the motions of a busy guy that's not really that busy at all.

WORKING FOR THE MAN RULE #9 • While it may feel good to tell a higher-level person that she's a "total fucking moron," it is most likely a bad idea that will probably get you fired.

So, what to do? How to get out from underneath the heap? How to keep from pulling your hair out? How to stop being at the office well after seven o'clock while your boss has left the building, sipped $12 cocktails at a posh bar, and then taken a cab home, leaving you to wait for the subway and wonder if the Laundromat's last load is 8:30 or 9 p.m.?

Reverse the slam. It takes some strategic thinking, and some planning, but once you get used to the game, it will seem like second nature. The key is to beat him to the punch, so that instead of your boss doling out orders and requests, you burden him with an avalanche of questions and requests for clarifications. As soon as you get to the office, immediately start firing away emails to your boss—asking questions and seeking direction regarding all the important tasks at hand. If he's off-site at a meeting, call his cell phone several times, asking a question each time.

Your boss will spend so much time responding to your questions that he won't have time to make so many requests. Of course you'll still be burdened with crazy demands, but you'll definitely lighten your own load. The gravy is that as your load lightens, your boss's plate gets fuller.

Questions to ask via email
- How did the meeting go? What in our proposal did the group respond to?
- Will you be here on Friday, or will you be off-site?
- Should we bring in Vendor X and Vendor Y on the same day?
- What time should we bring in Vendor X?
- What time should we bring in Vendor Y?
- When does our contract with Vendor X end? Should we think about bringing in new vendors?
- Will you be here after lunch today?

WORKING FOR THE MAN
RULE #10 • It's safer to say something that makes the same point without your boss realizing that you are actually making such a point. Something like "You know, you really remind me of [insert name of some obscure person from your life that you really, really despise]."

- Will you have time to go over that report I turned in?
- Should I add this paragraph to the report?
- Should we invite Mark and Sally to the meeting?
- Should we arrange a conference call with the West Coast team to discuss this issue, or was this handled in the meeting you went to yesterday?
- Who should I distribute the report to?

> **WORKING FOR THE MAN**
> **RULE #11** • The shorter the message, the more trouble that you're in. "Call me as soon as you get in" is bad. "See me" is really bad.

- Did you want me to send the report to Janice? She's not on your distribution list, but I believe you said in an earlier meeting that you wanted Janice involved every step of the way.
- I'll be finishing my report at 5:30. Will you be here to review?

RED PEN ANALYSIS

Your job involves writing letters and reports for your boss. These reports and letters go through a series of drafts, always marked up by a red pen, because your boss likes to make changes. Even simple three-line thank-you notes or confirmation memos will come back drenched in red ink, with ridiculous, petty corrections.

Don't go crazy. Don't quit. Don't jump out that window. Don't throw that stapler in your boss's general direction. Instead, master your mind-fuck capabilities.

You know your boss is going to make corrections, no matter how perfect your work. So leave two or three glaring mistakes—on purpose! Give it to your boss for review, but already have the corrected version ready to go.

How much do you want to bet that the only things marked up are the errors you purposefully left in the work? And does that mean you quickly turn over the corrected version that you already have at the ready? Of course not. How good it will feel to know that you don't have to do a damn thing, but

> **WORKING FOR THE MAN**
> **RULE #12 •** The time you finally lose it and begin to curse out the idiot who pissed all over the toilet seat, not to mention all the idiots you have to work with, as well as the idiotic company they, and you, work for, you will emerge from the stall to find the CEO of the company at the sink, washing his hands and staring at you through the reflection in the bathroom mirror.

your boss is sitting in his office waiting for you to come back in with a revised version based on *his* corrections, all the while you're kicking back and trying to decide which new album to buy from Amazon.com. Wait as long as you can before handing over the perfect version that you could have turned in literally two seconds after he gave you corrections.

Make it even more interesting by making copies of the paperwork and having coworkers place bets on which errors your boss will mark up. The person who marks up the paper just like your boss wins—call it "The Red Pen Challenge."

BOSS LETTERS (THE OPPOSITE OF LOVE LETTERS)

Save and collect all the absurd emails from your boss. When the time is right—probably when you have given your two weeks' notice after finding a better job—bind them up and make copies. Use the company copy center. Then, on your last day, leave copies here and there, and make sure a coworker passes along a copy to the new person who takes over your job.

WORST BOSS EVER

Document the experience of your worst boss ever. You have no idea how therapeutic it can be just to write out all the crap you had (or have) to deal with—all the belittling comments, the yelling and screaming, the name-calling, the micromanaging, the red-pen letters, the passive-aggressive power plays, the demeaning demands, the sexist comments, the condescension, the taking of credit for the work you slaved over, the blame thrown in your direction when things went wrong. With the worst boss ever, the list goes on and on and on.

Writing about your past experiences with former bosses can help you let go of any anger you may still be harboring. Why let the reign of terror continue, however slight? You already gave up so much of your headspace to these various bosses, it's important to get them out of there for good. You will also reveal some insights into how to better deal with these types of people, which will most certainly come in handy as you make your way through your very long professional arc.

If you are writing in the present tense, meaning that you are writing about the boss that is at this very moment making your life miserable, it will (1) be helpful in terms of stepping outside of the

WORKING FOR THE MAN RULE #13 • This time, when he asks your name (for the millionth time), he's unfortunately going to remember it.

current situation and putting some distance between you and the stress your boss is zapping into your tensed-up muscles, and (2) it might just be the eye-opener you need to actually start job hunting, something you are always talking about doing but never actually delve into. Is looking at a job site and sending out your résumé actually harder than dealing with the worst boss ever?

MEMO
boss case studies

There are all kinds of bosses out there, but they all have one thing in common: no matter what your boss's specific character flaws are, no matter how outrageous his or her behavior, no matter how annoying his or her petty demands, you work for your boss, and therefore have to put up with his or her reign of terror. The better you understand your boss and the particulars of his or her damage, the easier it will be to actually deal with your boss on a daily basis. Following are some common boss types that you have either worked for in the past or have a good chance of toiling under in the future.

The Could You Get Me a Cup of Coffee Boss

Every time you leave the office to get some fresh air, your boss will stop you and ask that you pick her up a cup of coffee, or a bagel, or a banana, something. Usually, she says she will pay you back, but never remembers to actually hand over any cash.

The List of Things for You to Do Boss

This boss spends most of his time either writing or dictating a list of things for you to accomplish. He will refer constantly to the list, and ask about particular items over and over again, even if you've explained that those items were completed days ago.

The Do I Have Any Messages Boss

Your boss spends lots of time outside of the office, at meetings, or traveling on business trips, but instead of being able to enjoy the unsupervised time, you have to deal with constant calls from your boss. She wants to know if she has any messages. You find yourself constantly on edge every time the phone rings. And once you give her the messages, she barks out orders about how to respond to the various calls.

The Change This One Thing Boss

You complete your work and do a bang-up job—as close to flawless as possible. You know it and your coworkers know it, and your boss knows it, too. But your boss needs to feel like he has contributed to the work, and so he asks that you "change this one thing."

The Reader of Pop Psychology Business Books Boss

Your boss starts using a new word that sounds phony in almost every conversation. The new word is used incessantly until it is replaced by another new word. Also, your boss occasionally implements new employee programs in an attempt to improve morale (and therefore worker productivity). The programs reek of formulaic unoriginality (blue sky morning meetings, team puzzle-making sessions, crazy tie day, build your own ice-cream sundae) and usually inspire nothing more than contempt from the workers.

The Let's Win Boss

He never played football, but in his mind your boss was the star quarterback of—at the very minimum—his high school varsity team. He sends out regular emails full of go-go rah-rah sports clichés, encouraging the idea that we are all on the same team, and we are working together "to win." Occasionally, he walks around checking in with people and offering encouraging words, as if he's moving along the sidelines talking to players during a close game. And twice a year, he holds court at an all-hands meeting that is more like a rally, with everyone clapping and cheering bullet point, presentation-only successes. All of these measures certainly inspire, but probably not in the way the boss intends. People don't feel victorious—they feel ridiculous, and have nothing but contempt for the boss who forces them, either literally or figuratively, to high-five "wins" that are nothing more than phony, unmoving motivational ploys.

The Big Show Boss

Your boss doesn't ever make any money for the company, nor does she actually ever deliver what she's promised, but she is the master of big presentations. She knows how to get management to buy in, and she knows how to make it seem like what she got them to buy is the best thing they've ever invested in, even though it's all total bullshit. You know this because it's so obvious to those on the so-called factory floor, but also because you helped her prepare the Power-Point slides. All fluff and puff and unrealistically rosy visions of the future. You learned early on not to ask questions about actual revenue, how many units have been sold, how many clients have signed up, or how many customers have subscribed. And you certainly don't bring up any targets from past presentations—because those are never actually met.

The Throw You Under the Bus Boss

Your boss always makes a point of telling you that he's protecting you and looking out for you, calling you into his office to regale you with stories about how he went to bat for you with upper management and in the bigwig meetings. But eventually you learn from other sources and confidants that your boss uses you to explain failures and disappointments that he is responsible for. Note that the more often your boss tells you that he's protecting you, the more he is actually selling you out.

The Ask a Question That He Already Knows the Answer to Boss

Your boss, in order to make himself feel like he's too important to be troubled with minor details, will constantly ask you, the lowly worker bee, questions about items for which he most certainly knows the answers—things like the date of a certain event or the name of a person he recently met with. Usually, he will do this in front of someone he is trying to impress.

The It's Five O'clock on Friday But I Really Need You to Get This Done Boss

Without fail, your boss will always drop assignments in your lap at the last possible minute, completely disregarding any plans you might have, not to mention quitting time.

The Let's Have a Quick Meeting Boss

Your boss doesn't actually do anything, so in order to fill this void and give the false sense that she is actually necessary, she constantly calls meetings. At these meetings she will go over things that have already been decided, so she knows "where everyone is at," and then waste considerable amounts of time wondering out loud if there is "anything else we should be doing." No one says anything, or offers up any new ideas—you're all too worried about the work already on your plates that you aren't able to get done due to all the time being wasted in pointless meetings.

more boss rules

WORKING FOR THE MAN RULE #14 • The longer the message on your voice mail, the less important it is: "Hey, Harry, sorry to call again, but I wanted to mention one last detail about tomorrow's noon meeting, which is in the big conference room on your floor, the eighteenth . . . Oh wait, they moved you guys, okay, well, anyway, on the eighteenth floor in the big conference room, we'll be discussing not just the monthly report figures, but we're gonna have a little brainstorming session at the tail end of the meeting on how to be more proactive on all the initiatives that were discussed in the most recent management meeting . . . If you need a copy of the summary report on that management meeting, give Gina, Jim's assistant, a call. She'll get you the document, either by email or she'll walk over a copy, however you want it, but if you don't have it, you should really get a copy. Anyway, so, this is just a heads-up on all that, so you can do a little pre-thinking before the meeting. Not sure if we'll be getting lunch, but hopefully, you know, since it's a noon meeting, we'll get those sandwiches again. Those were some great sandwiches. Okay, well . . . Oh, wait, just one more thing . . ."

WORKING FOR THE MAN RULE #15 • After you've poured yourself the last cup of joe, the big boss will walk in—with empty coffee mug swinging—just in time to witness the one time you've decided to duck out of making a new pot of coffee.

WORKING FOR THE MAN RULE #16 • On the days that you show up late, you will end up in the elevator on the way up to your office with your boss, who decided to step out, after having already been at work for hours, to grab her third morning cup of coffee.

WORKING FOR THE MAN RULE #17 • "I'm working from home" actually means "I've decided to stay home so I can take care of personal shit, like bills, laundry, changing the cat litter, and watching the morning talk shows."

WORKING FOR THE MAN RULE #18 • Though it's not an option for you, your boss will call to say she is "working from home" as often as once a week. Though you will despise her because you know damn well she isn't doing any work at all, you will also savor the fact that she's out of the office and you don't have to see her face.

WORKING FOR THE MAN RULE #19 • Unfortunately, your boss will probably make her presence felt by calling in every hour or so—speaking in an overly authoritative manner—to create the appearance that she is hard at work even though she is not in the office. Each call will bring your blood to a boil.

WORKING FOR THE MAN RULE #20 • Your boss will tell you, often in an overly dramatic fashion, that he wants you to be innovative. What he really means is that he wants you to come up with innovative ideas that he can take credit for.

WORKING FOR THE MAN RULE #21 • If you happen to go around your boss with a solid, innovative idea, and therefore get all the credit for yourself, don't expect any rewards or a promotion. In fact, you are guaranteed but one thing: a smackdown.

WORKING FOR THE MAN RULE #22 • Accolades in the office are few and far between because they involve one key ingredient: making your boss look good.

WORKING FOR THE MAN RULE #23 • No one likes to make his or her boss look good.

oworkers. Can't live with them, but there they are, all around you. The worse your day is, the more around you they will feel, hovering like a shadeless summer day, laughing annoyingly at stupid jokes, popping by at inopportune moments, slurping soup loudly. It's sort of like prison, or a family reunion at a remote beach house, or taking a cruise with the spouse *and* the in-laws.

Life in the office is defined less by the work that you do than by the people you work with—all the personalities; the

**WORKING FOR THE MAN
RULE #24** • Never trust
anyone who uses exclamation
points in email correspondence: "This is great! I really
appreciate your work on getting
this going! I look forward
to working with you on this
project!"

mood swings; each person's unique displays of dissatisfaction, unhappiness, and stress. While it can certainly be a recipe for disaster—passive aggressive boilovers, petty backstabbing, and worst of the worst, scissor and stapler stealing—there are ways to make dealing with your coworkers not only tolerable, but downright fun. Don't get mad, get inspired.

to-do list

COWORKER FICTION

Coworker fiction is just like fan fiction, except the characters are your coworkers and you're the author. One story could involve that coworker who brushes his teeth in the bathroom, and doesn't rinse out the sink afterward, so all his sudsy toothpaste waste is covering the basin. Well, in real life, you can't grab the back of his head and smash his face in the sink, where you then rub his hopefully broken nose in his own disgusting toothpaste spit. But in fan, I mean, coworker fiction, it's wide open! Beat that fucker to a bloody, toothpaste-sudsy pulp.

OPTION: Collaborate with a trusted coworker via instant message. In typical IM fashion, flinging instantaneous messages back and forth as fast as you can type them, you'll bang out a story in no time.

To get you started:

- Your coworker goes into her office every day at the exact same time and closes the door for exactly eleven minutes. What is she doing in there?
- Everyone had left the office, or so you thought. Walking through the darkened halls to get a glass of water and see about making a fresh pot of coffee, you saw something that you most definitely should not have seen . . .
- There's one coworker who buys lunch every day but doesn't finish it. Instead of throwing it away, he puts it in the fridge, where it remains until it rots and stinks up the office. Everyone in the office decides to teach him a lesson he, or at least his nose, will never forget . . .

WORKING FOR THE MAN RULE #25 • These are the things you immediately know about people who say "my assistant" more than once in a short conversation: They're insecure, their job sucks, and they've got a small dick (this applies to both men and women).

- That guy in the corner doesn't actually do any work. What he does all day is this . . .
- Everyone gathers in the conference room for drinks after work. No one has had a good day. Everyone is having more than one, then two, then three . . . Out come the true feelings. There's lots of laughter, until someone says a little too much . . .

EMPLOYEE OF THE MONTH

The Employee of the Month Award should be a great way for management to recognize an employee each month for his or her excellent work. In reality, HR sends countless emails each month trying to get someone's assistant to get an okay on whomever it is they are trying to push through as the winner—usually some lower-level cog in the machine who, instead of getting a raise for his good work, is given a pathetic certificate (from an office supply store) and possibly a gift certificate.

Why should management get to hand out all the spoils? They have no clue what's going on in the trenches anyway. And why does the Employee of the Month have to be given to someone based on so-called excellence? What about that tool who totally fucked up? The guy who left his window open, caused the pipes to freeze and then burst, and created a flood on the seventeenth and eighteenth floors of the building? What about the salesperson that included a client on a Reply to All email in which she called said client a moron who wouldn't know a good proposal from a hole in her head, thereby losing a major account? What about the dude who showed up to an important meeting, late, no less, not realizing he was the one who was supposed to make the presentation? Employees of the Month, all of them.

Buy the same certificates your

WORKING FOR THE MAN
RULE #26 • A quick way to freak out a coworker is to tell him that they are going to move the copy machine right outside of his cube.

company uses, and hand out your own Employee of the Month awards. And there doesn't have to be just one Employee of the Month—to be so stingy would be more in the spirit of management. Everyone who deserves a certificate should get one.

PEOPLE TO KISS UP TO

There's no doubt that you hate tons of people in your office—they range from your boss to the lowly assistant on a floor you don't even work on. And whatever it is that they do to cause you to dislike them, you could list them out in no time at all. Your significant other at home could probably list them out as well, since you bitch and moan about them all the time.

And while that would be a fun list to write, especially if you added caricature drawings and some of the more ridiculous words that have come out of those people's mouths, the list that will do you more good is one that comprises the people you should kiss up to (sort of like the opposite of an Enemies List). Who should be on this list? Anyone who can help you out or has or does something that you need or want. This list will serve not only as a directory of who can help you do what, but also as a reminder of who to be nice to, even if they don't deserve such nicety. Following are some office personnel who you might consider putting on your list.

Tech Support. These guys can get you the software you need, and other types of computer programs and perks. Plus, you'll be a priority to get upgrades and fixes, even if you aren't really a priority in the office scheme of things. And when your home computer breaks down, these guys won't mind helping you out.

The Finance Manager. He approves things like new computers. Make sure you aren't the last one to get a flat-screen monitor.

Mail Room. Need to overnight your Mom's Mother's Day gift, a thirty-pound something or other? The guys in the mail room will take care of it for you—free of charge, that is—if you're good to them. Or at the very least, they won't alert your boss that you are sending expensive packages via the office mail system.

WORKING FOR THE MAN RULE #28 • If you witness a guy in the bathroom who takes a leak and then walks out without washing his hands, you will never be able to think of anything else when you see him walking around the office. Also, you will feel compelled to tell other people. You wish you could send a note about the matter to "Office All."

Building Manager. Don't get on this person's bad list with complaints about whether it's too cold or hot. The building manager usually handles cubicle and office moves and other types of things that can seriously impact your life in the office. Be good to this person to insure that you don't end up in the cube next to the bathroom, the reception area, or a copy machine.

The Salespeople. While they may be the worst, salespeople know how the company is really doing. They know what money is—or is not—coming in. They have a nose for knowing who is important and on their way up. Get close and they'll fill you in—they love to brag about their "insider" information.

Your Boss's Boss. For one thing, it will drive your immediate boss crazy if you're on good terms with her boss. Second, your boss may eventually become executive fat that gets cut—if you're on good terms with the person whose left standing, you may just save your job.

The People Who Get Sent Swag. Certain people in the office are known for getting sent valuable, or at least hearty, swag, usually the folks who buy from the high-level vendors, or from any of the start-ups who are at the moment flush with cash. Identify the receivers of these gifts—everything from cookies to fruit baskets to tickets to sporting events—so that you may possibly get in on the action.

The Person Who Regularly Brings in Homemade Baked Goods. You definitely want this person stopping by your cubicle offering the latest of whatever it is she has baked.

The Executive Assistants Who Order (And Then Clear Out) Catered Lunches. To guarantee that they won't run out of food at big meetings or meetings that involve bigwigs, the assistants who take care of bringing in all the

WORKING FOR THE MAN RULE #29 • If you have a coworker that uses a made up, annoying word, such as "ridonkulous" (as in, "That's ridonkulous!") all the time, you may find, much to your chagrin (and that of your significant other, as well), that you start using the word as well. Isn't that ridonkulous?

**WORKING FOR THE MAN
RULE #30** • If people in your office are really annoying you, burn some popcorn in the office microwave.

trays of sandwiches, salads, bags of chips, and beverages always order too much of everything. If you are nice, they'll let you know when the leftovers can be picked apart and where they are located. There may be no such thing as a free lunch, but there is definitely such a thing as good sandwiches that you don't have to pay for.

INTEROFFICE MAIL

Don't you just love getting interoffice mail from a person just one floor above you who you see all the time—or better yet, from someone on the same floor, just a stress ball's throw away?

But I understand why people use it—interoffice mail allows you to get information to coworkers without actually having to speak with them. So why not have some fun with these mailers? Send your coworkers nonsensical notes, correspondence with a year-old date, a memo from a despised former coworker who is *not* back at the company, urgent reports that have nothing to do with them, or a flagged magazine article with a title like, "What to Do When All Your Coworkers Hate You."

Just make sure you use mailers that don't have your name on them, no matter how high up on the list of penned-up names.

MEMO
coworker case studies

Of course you can't stand them, because they're petty, annoying, abrasive, make you feel small, gross you out, and in general, drive you crazy. Instead of stewing in agitated disbelief, wondering what it is you did in a past life to deserve this sorry nine-to-never-ending existence with such a sorry lot of ridiculously obnoxious coworkers, definitively define their grating attributes in grueling detail, and if you've got the knack for caricature, or heck, even if you can only muster stick figure artistry, why not throw in pictures to fully capture exactly what it is that makes you want to either (1) beat someone to a pulp, or (2) get a running start and hurl yourself out the window.

The Is It Friday Yet Guy

You see this guy first thing Monday morning on the elevator; he looks you square in the eyes and asks, "Is it Friday yet?" He's not looking for an answer, just commiseration. "I know," you say, "I know . . ." It's just small-talk office banter. Except this guy is like a broken record. See him in the hall later in the day, he asks the question again. In the bathroom, the jokey question is thrown at you as you quickly try to slam the stall door shut. When he stops by your desk, boom, there it is again. He thinks he's a real laugh riot. The questioning goes on all week. On Fridays, he thinks he's *really* funny. "Is it Friday yet?" he asks, and you say, "Yes, it is! Thank goodness." Thank goodness the "Is it Friday yet?" questioning is over for the week.

The Thong Panties Chick

It's not just revealed as she bends over when she's wearing her low-cut jeans—you can see her thong strap pretty much all the time, no matter what she's wearing or how she's positioned. White pants, red thong. Black pants, white thong. Tight skirt or tight pants—the attire that gave rise to the thong in the first place in order to disappear a panty line— and there it is, strap pulled up just high enough to peek out and reveal itself. But even a hint of a thong strap is actually a scream that is loudly exclaiming, "LOOK AT MY FINE ASS!" This girl ain't trying to hide a thing. She wants to make sure you *know* that she's wearing a thong.

The Tanning Booth Betty

At first you think she's just gotten back from a Caribbean island vacation. But then you realize the look is constant, week after week. She can't possibly be jetting off for a beach vacation every weekend. The constant state of her tan makes you take a harder look, and you notice the orange glow, the unnatural look of the darkened skin. It reminds you of a bad paint job, where the person not only bought the wrong shade of a bad color, but decided to purchase the cheapest stuff on the shelf as well.

The Watcha Doin' Chick

Always comes at the most inopportune moments, while you are either on deadline, or working diligently on your own stuff, and not in the mood for small talk, and asks, in that obnoxiously bubbly way, "Watcha doin'?" Of course she's not sexy—if that were the case, you'd be thrilled by the attention and thanking your lucky stars. She's annoying and spacey, the kind of person who you not only wonder what it is exactly that she does, but how she ever got hired in the first place. You stare straight at your computer and give yes-or-no and finally just rude nodding-head answers, but she still doesn't leave. *What am I doing? Wishing you would just shut up and get the hell away from me.*

The Ask for It Guy

Of all the people in your office, this is the guy to watch. He doesn't work that hard. He shows up late and leaves early. Sometimes he doesn't show up at all. He responds to urgent emails weeks after they were sent. He does get his work done, though it's not particularly amazing or groundbreaking. And yet, he seems to always be on an upwardly mobile path—getting that nicer office, the plum assignments, the invitations to sought-after lunches or golf outings, and—most painfully—seemingly accelerated promotions. How in the fuck does this guy do it? Because he *asks* for it. It really is that simple. Whereas most people have that little voice inside them that says, "You don't deserve it," and keep their heads down and their mouths shut, he's got the total opposite ringing in his ears: "I deserve it, I was born to have it, it shouldn't be any other way, only a fool would deny me." It doesn't occur to him that he is undeserving or possibly asking out of turn, and he doesn't miss a single opportunity to ask for whatever it is that he wants. Don't kill this person. Don't stalk him in the parking garage and club him with a tire iron. Watch and learn and try to emulate. You may hate yourself for becoming the Ask for It Guy, but at least you'll be hating yourself while sitting in a nicer office and making more money.

The Bitchy Queen

Her smile gives it away. It's fake. Even the most oblivious dude in the office can pick up on it. It's that obvious. She never really yells, or says anything mean in a direct way, but after you speak with her and turn around to leave, you get the distinct feeling that she's pulled out a knife and is about to stab you—not once, but like fifty times. She's risen up the chain and she's high-level—laughing with the big boys. They're probably scared of her, too. You never know what she really thinks—she's always flashing that smile, which you know is fake. But is it bad fake, or good fake? No real way to tell, and it would be pointless to know the truth anyway, because she's already sized you up and chewed up your escape routes. Know that you are no match for her and keep your eyes on her hands. Your back is already up against the wall, so at least you'll see it coming.

The Phil Mickelson Wannabe

He wears suits Monday through Thursday, but on Fridays, his true calling and identity is revealed: khaki pants and a golf shirt (from a tournament that he played in, no less!). He talks golf eight days a week, but gets to dress the part on casual Friday. He has a putting machine in his office, and when he's on the phone, he uses a headset so that he can putt around. During staff meetings that he leads, that putter is his staff. He uses the head of the club to point at people. *Are we running a golf tournament?* you think to yourself. *Are we in the golf club business? Do we manage pro golfers? Sell golf carts?* No, your company has nothing to do with golf, you just work for a Phil Mickelson Wannabe. What can you do? Not much. But canceling the golf channel from your cable bill might make you feel better.

The Hey Everyone, I'm Going to Take a Dump Guy

It happens like clockwork, usually right after the morning cup of coffee or right after lunch. You look up and there he is, ambling his way down the hallway, a face that says both *I'm relaxed and at ease* and *Don't have time to talk, got to get to where I'm going.* But the dead giveaway is the magazine tucked under his arm. No file folders or laptop. Just a magazine. Everyone's got to take a dump, but this guy has to let the whole world know. And it's always a guy. Never a woman.

NOTE: If you are ever in this guy's office and happen to see a magazine with a cover story that catches your eye, don't mention that you'd like to read it. He'll offer to loan you his copy, and of course, that's the last thing you want to have to touch. You know exactly where it's been.

The I Would Just Bend Her Over Dude

This guy is always loitering around, at your cube, out in front of the building, in line at the busy sandwich shop at lunchtime. You don't want to be hanging out with him, but there he is, near you, making one particular observation every time a semi-decent hot chick walks by: "I would just bend her over . . ." His physical lean in implies he's sort of whispering you a secret, but the sound of his voice is booming loud enough for not only the girl to hear what he's saying, but other people standing nearby as well. You sort of smile uncomfortably, hoping no one is bothering to listen, and quickly change the subject to something mundane, like the weather. "Nice day out, huh," you say, all the while thinking that you just want this schlub—who ain't bending anyone over anytime soon—to get the fuck away from you.

Suggestion: Instead of responding with a change of subject, say this: "Of course—you'll need her back to support your fat stomach."

The Yankees Fan

It could be any team, really, but your guy happens to be a Yankees fan. He knows the team like those guys who sit in the bleachers and talk about a game from twenty years ago like it was yesterday. So confident he is in his team, he'll take any bet, no matter how desperate the situation is for the Yankees. Maybe you don't know anything about the Yankees, or you want to see them lose just because they're never the underdog, or you're not in the mood to talk baseball, but there is the Yankees Fan, asking if you saw the game last night and if you want to place a bet on the game tonight. At least he isn't asking you about work. If you think about it that way, he's not such a bad guy to talk to after all.

The Who's That Guy Dude

This dude has no long-term memory, *and* he's paranoid. Every time he sees someone he doesn't recognize, which is pretty much everyone he doesn't work with on a daily basis, he leans in as if conducting a drug deal and asks, "Who's that guy?" like he thinks the guy is a cop or something. "That's Jim, the IT guy," you say. "He's been here for *years*." "Oh, right," your paranoid friend says, and then goes back to whatever it was that he was blathering on about. Eventually, you get tired of him asking you who everyone is. To stop it, just start responding with this: "That's the guy that they're thinking of bringing in to manage you." Or "That's the guy that's interviewing for your job . . . Better start dusting off your résumé!"

The What's His Title Guy

This guy never lets you finish a sentence when you bring someone up around the office. He's less interested in what you are talking about than *who* you are talking about, specifically what the person's title is.

You: "So I was talking to Jim about how we might be able to—"

What's His Title? Guy: "Jim? Jim who? What's his title?"

If the person's title is lower than his, then he rolls his eyes and acts like he had that idea four years ago, or says, as if he's the guy to give the nod of approval, "Pretty good, pretty good. Needs some work, but pretty good." If the guy's title is above his, he laughs nervously, like he's forcing it, and says, "That's the dumbest thing I've ever heard." He then repeats the same basic sentiment over and over in slightly different variations:

"My kid could have come up with that one."

"These upper management dudes, they don't know jack shit."

"No wonder this company is going to hell."

"I'll tell you, I've worked at a lot of places, and these guys are the absolute worst."

"If I were in charge, boy . . . If I were in charge . . . Let's just say I could do better blindfolded."

The Could You Do Me A Favor Chick

She comes over and says hello like she's been really looking forward to seeing you all day, like she's a friend. Of
course, you know the score. You didn't always know the
score, but it's the ol' "fool me once, shame on you, fool me
twice, shame on me" kind of situation. She knows that you
know, but that doesn't stop her little act. She does the
small talk thing so well, like she actually cares how you
are doing. She seems to really be listening to the nothing
words coming out of your mouth. You really don't do so
well when you're talking to her, because your mind is trying to zero in on when she's going to slice in so perfectly
and effortlessly the "Could you do me a favor?" question.
She does it so expertly that even though you know it's
coming, even though she's done it a million times before,
even though you've practiced saying no over two million
times in your head, you find yourself agreeing to help her
out. Of course she's a babe, yes, but she's not interested in
you and you know it, yet there you go, nodding your head
like a little puppy dog, like you are back in high school
doing the bidding of bitchy Christie the cheerleader in her
short floppy skirt. Sucker. You are a sucker. You were born
a sucker and you will be a sucker till the day you die.

more coworker rules

WORKING FOR THE MAN RULE #31 • If people in your office are really, really annoying you, burn some leftover fish in the office microwave.

WORKING FOR THE MAN RULE #32 • Understand that when someone says, "Oh, is this bothering you?" it means, "Fuck you."

WORKING FOR THE MAN RULE #33 • Learn how to say, "Oh, is this bothering you?" with just the right pitch.

WORKING FOR THE MAN RULE #34 • The guys with framed eight-by-ten photos of their wives in their offices are the ones who fuck around.

WORKING FOR THE MAN RULE #35 • The dork who wears a brown belt with black shoes, khaki pants, and those deep blue dress shirts a size too big never, ever has a girlfriend, but he's always, always looking.

WORKING FOR THE MAN RULE #36 • That's the guy who's going to ask you out.

WORKING FOR THE MAN RULE #37 • The hot girl in the office who wears the short skirts and sexy boots always, always has a boyfriend.

WORKING FOR THE MAN RULE #38 • If a salesperson says, "I need a decision, 100K is on the line!" you can assume that means a few thousand dollars, and there is no real urgency to the matter.

WORKING FOR THE MAN RULE #39 • If a salesperson says, "I need a decision, 10K is on the line!" you don't need to get back to him at all.

WORKING FOR THE MAN RULE #40 • The job title "Marketing Coordinator" is interchangeable with "The Sales Team's Bitch."

WORKING FOR THE MAN RULE #41 • The top salesman in your office always seems to have "a family emergency" on Fridays, especially when the weather gets nice.

WORKING FOR THE MAN RULE #42 • This does compute: The top salesman in your office will go to four funerals over the course of the year, all for his grandmother.

WORKING FOR THE MAN RULE #43 • Next year, the funerals will be for his grandfather.

WORKING FOR THE MAN RULE #44 • The year after that, the salesman will start back over with funerals for his grandmother.

WORKING FOR THE MAN RULE #45 • After the nuclear war, it won't just be cockroaches left to roam the earth. There will also be salesmen, selling things to each other.

WORKING FOR THE MAN RULE #46 • If a certain coworker is getting on your nerves, go up to him and say, "Hey, there are all these sandwiches and cookies and pasta salads in the kitchen—someone had leftovers from a big meeting." Of course, there's nothing in the kitchen but the crappy offerings in the vending machine. He'll come back and say, "What are you talking about? There was nothing there." And you'll just say, "Oh, man, I guess it all already got eaten up."

WORKING FOR THE MAN RULE #47 • The "Hey, there are all these sandwiches" ruse is especially effective if you use it right after your annoying coworker has said, "Oh man, I'm really hungry."

WORKING FOR THE MAN RULE #48 • Every office has two women who sit together and hang out together, and can be perfectly defined as "The Two Biddies."

WORKING FOR THE MAN RULE #49 • If Biddy #1 happens to be away from her desk, and you ask Biddy #2 if she knows where Biddy #1 might be, Biddy #2 will give you a hateful, menacing glare and hiss, "How should I know?"

WORKING FOR THE MAN RULE #50 • An unsigned note that says "Please don't make the coffee too strong" will occasionally be posted near the coffeemaker. You can bet your bottom dollar that The Two Biddies wrote it.

WORKING FOR THE MAN RULE #51 • You know to avoid conversation with a coworker when you overhear him saying, "I was listening to Rush Limbaugh . . ." Or, if you're on the other side of the political fence: "I was listening to Janeane Garofalo . . ." Or, because this is a very similar scenario that you really don't want to listen to: "My stomach is in turmoil . . . I was in the bathroom all night!"

WORKING FOR THE MAN RULE #52 • The most disheveled, gruff guy in the office is the one who says to you, as often as he can, "Somebody sure got up on the wrong side of the bed this morning."

WORKING FOR THE MAN RULE #53 • One morning, you really will have woken up on the "wrong side of the bed," and after this guy makes his broken record comment, you will say, "Hey, Fuckface, you're ugly, you dress like shit, you stink, and no one likes you—and that's when you get up on the *right* side of the bed."

WORKING FOR THE MAN RULE #54 • There is always that one guy in the office who likes to brag about his terrible taste in music. "Guess which album I just bought?" he asks relentlessly, not letting up until you say, "What'd you buy?" He responds with two thumbs-up, his smile as big as a house: "Air Supply's *Greatest Hits*, baby. Rock on!"

WORKING FOR THE MAN RULE #55 • This same guy often ends his statements with "You know you love it!" when in fact, no, you don't. You feel quite the opposite.

WORKING FOR THE MAN RULE #56 • The passive-aggressive psycho you dated and broke up with in that year after college is the woman in your office who makes sure, when emailing you, to CC your boss in order not only to get what she wants, but to try to make you look bad as well.

WORKING FOR THE MAN RULE #57 • There's a guy who you will always see in the bathroom, and every time, he will complain about how people piss all over the seats. "People are just so disgusting . . . I'm going to put up some signs," he says. You say, "Yeah, you should do that." He replies, "Yeah, I am gonna put up some signs." Of course he never puts up any signs.

WORKING FOR THE MAN RULE #58 • The are a lot of idiots in your office, but the guy who recommends to coworkers that they read *Who Moved My Cheese?* is most definitely office idiot #1.

WORKING FOR THE MAN RULE #59 • There's always a guy at the office who will come up to you and say, "What, is it St. Patrick's Day?" if you happen to be wearing an outfit that is mostly green.

WORKING FOR THE MAN RULE #60 • Giving your annoying coworker—who is *not* your secretary—a big bouquet of flowers on Secretary's Day, certainly won't improve your working relationship, but it will definitely provide a nice lift to *your* day.

WORKING FOR THE MAN RULE #61 • A great way to gauge your coworkers is to post a sign in your cube that says, "I ALWAYS GIVE 110%" in big block letters. People who commend you should be shunned. (For example, the higher-up sales asshole will probably say, "I like the way you think," as if he is your commanding officer.) The people who call you on your bullshit, those are the folks you want to grab drinks with after work.

WORKING FOR THE MAN RULE #62 • It's best to avoid getting teamed up on a project with an "I saw the movie but didn't read the book" kind of guy.

WORKING FOR THE MAN RULE #63 • If your coworker is always asking you about whether or not you got a bonus, just tell him that yes, you did get a bonus, and that it was far bigger than you expected. Tell him that your boss said that not everyone would be getting a bonus—only those who management felt deserved one. Of course you didn't get a bonus, but at least your coworker will stop asking whether or not you got one.

WORKING FOR THE MAN RULE #64 • If your coworker won't shut up about not getting a bonus, stop by his cubicle every once in a while and say, "Oh, hey, the CEO stopped by and wanted to give you your bonus." Then, drop a penny on his desk.

WORKING FOR THE MAN RULE #65 • After you do the penny joke one too many times, change it up and deepen the insult by placing a Canadian penny on your coworker's desk.

WORKING FOR THE MAN RULE #66 • When your coworker decides to play the same joke on you, belittle him for being a copycat and tell him his total lack of originality and inability to think outside the box is probably the reason he did not get a bonus this year.

WORKING FOR THE MAN RULE #67 • If a coworker is getting on your nerves, start calling him by an obnoxious nickname. Tell people around the office the name you've coined for this particular person. See if you can make it stick.

WORKING FOR THE MAN RULE #68 • While you're at it, add that your coworker is trying get on the professional hot dog eating contest circuit. Say he just took runner-up at the country fair for the second year in a row.

WORKING FOR THE MAN RULE #69 • Even during one of those heart-to-heart coworker bonding sessions over how shitty your respective jobs are, never reveal how much money you make. If your coworker knows you make more money than he does, he will resent you. If he knows you make less than he does, he will treat you with less respect and feel superior to you.

WORKING FOR THE MAN RULE #70 • Even if you've been told by numerous reliable sources, do not ever ask a coworker if she is pregnant. Wait until she tells you.

WORKING FOR THE MAN RULE #71 • If you do make the mistake of asking this question to a woman that is not pregnant, don't even try to apologize. Just keep your mouth shut and walk away. There is nothing you can say, not then or in the future, that will repair the relationship. This not-pregnant woman is going to hate you forever.

CHAPTER THREE

Coworker Collaboration (Given the Cohabitation)

You're stuck with these folks whether you like it or not, hour after hour, day after day, in often miserable and stressed out conditions, so it would be foolish not to try to make the best of it. And who knows what kind of friendships might develop or what alliances can be forged, and what these relationships might lead to? You may end up becoming friends with a coworker who turns out to be dating a person that can help you land a better job in an area that you've been trying to break into, for example. Plus, the more the merrier principle holds, and there's also safety in numbers. You might not be able to throw an all-out party, but collectively you can certainly come up with unique and engaging ways to pass the time and have fun together while you're on the clock.

to-do list

START A ONE BOTTLE, ONE BAG OF ICE TRADITION

Get a bottle of liquor and a bag of ice and some cups. Then send around an email invite to a few key people—coworkers that you actually like—to come to a conference room, preferably one high up and with a nice view, at quitting time. Tell them it's the start of a new tradition—the One Bottle, One Bag of Ice Tradition.

At the inaugural gathering, make sure to give a toast.

Suggested toast: "To the grief."

Getting everyone together to have a drink is a great way to end the day, a great way to foster friendship among coworkers and collectively blow off some steam—something to actually look forward to. People can stop in for a quick drink before they dart off for home, or can sit around until the sun goes down and the bottle is drip dry.

Do it weekly, or monthly, or whenever someone calls up a gathering. Rotate who brings the bottle and the ice—and whoever brings the bottle gets to make the call on the beverage—scotch, whiskey, vodka, Jägermeister. Jägermeister, you ask, incredulous? Well just think of the stories that would come out after a bottle of Jägermeister.

NOTE: No mixers should be allowed.

NOTE: It's your tradition, so do whatever you want.

Warning: Your company probably has a rule against drinking alcohol in the building. As long as your gatherings don't get too big, you most likely won't have any problems. But if they get big, or someone tells the wrong person (a tattletale—surely not someone that would be invited), or your boss has been looking for an easy way to show cause to have you fired, you could find yourself in a bit of a jam, or more precisely, out of a job.

CREATE THE CHARLES BUKOWSKI BOOK GROUP

Form a book group at work. But forget all the typical business book drivel. The reading of such books would mean one or more of the following:

- You are not only reading a terrible book but further lining the pockets of an overpaid CEO (who didn't even write the book in the first place—that's right, an underpaid ghostwriter, probably a freelancer who doesn't even work in an office, penned those words of corporate "wisdom").
- You are feeding your mind with nothing more than clichés.
- You are analyzing and "getting" nothing more than oversimplified explanations of efficiency and trend models. They may make you feel smart, but you aren't really getting that much smarter. If it hadn't been dumbed down, you probably would not be getting it.
- You are reading the exact same books that thousands of other worker hacks have got on their nightstands. If these books give you any new ideas or new

ways of thinking—they will not be original. You read the book like a sheep, and now you simply share the wisdom of the herd.

What books should you read? Yes, the name of your book group is the Charles Bukowski Book Group, and yes, you should most definitely inaugurate the first meeting with a discussion of *Post Office*, but you don't have to *only* read books by Bukowski. That being said, the sentiment of his body of work with regard to the world of work should be a consistent theme of your selections.

Some suggestions:

- **On the serious side:** *The Jungle* by Upton Sinclair; *Working* by Studs Terkel; *Animal Farm* by George Orwell; *Nickel and Dimed* by Barbara Ehrenreich
- **Well-written classics:** *The Water-Method Man* by John Irving; *Factotum* by Charles Bukowski (Yes, I know I mentioned that your Bukowski Book Group does not have to read *all* Bukowski books, but this is a must-read for those with a predilection for job-hopping. Indeed, this is the ultimate job-hopping book.); *Catch-22* by Joseph Heller
- **More recent entries to the workplace genre:** *Slab Rat* by Ted Heller; *Job Hopper* by Ayun Halliday; *The Devil Wears Prada* by Lauren Weisberger; *Then We Came to the End* by Joshua Ferris; *Everyday Life* by Lydie Salvayre; *The Mezzanine* by Nicholson Baker

FILM FESTIVAL

Throw a film festival at the office. Hold it during the lunch hour over the course of a few weeks. Split the movies in half— so each two-hour movie is shown over two consecutive days. Utilize one of the conference rooms—whether you've got a killer high-tech system with a huge flat-screen monitor, or just a basic television set with a built-in DVD player. Do the festival during the winter months, when everyone is either ordering in food or bringing a bag lunch because it's too damn cold to go outside. Just like any film festival, it's less about the venue and more about the film selections. Picking a theme is key, but given that you're holding this film festival at the office, it's really a no-brainer: The theme should be all about the workplace.

Here then, are some suggested selections:

- *Stripes*—That scene where he throws his taxicab keys off the bridge—beautiful. It just keeps getting better from there, and that's the opening sequence.
- *Office Space*—A classic. If we could all have such an attitudinal shift and be so heroic in the drear of our cube life.
- *9 to 5*—Oh, if only . . . A wonderful bit of early eighties fantasy. Nice rope contraptions.
- *Clerks*—At the end of the day, we're all just clerks, taking orders and punching keys.
- *Fear and Trembling*—Nice sequence in which the main character removes all her clothes and dances around the office in the middle of the night. Having

mentioned this, I know you are now adding it to, and moving it up to the top of, your Netflix queue. But note, this is a very dark, rather depressing film about a woman who starts out working at a desk and ends up as the bathroom attendant.

- *Party Girl*—The story of a sexy party girl/reluctant library clerk. Nothing like a sexy party girl working in a library.

- *Ikiru*—A serious film. This one makes you take a hard look in the mirror. Guaranteed to influence the way you look at your working life.

- *Swimming with Sharks*—If you recognize your boss in any way, time to get the hell out. Don't even wait until the credits roll. Get up, clear out your desk, walk out the door, and don't look back.

- *Clockwatchers*—A very thoughtful and eye-opening look at being a temp, how the detachment of temp work can create a displaced sense of self-worth.

- *How to Get Ahead in Advertising*—A fantastical look at how the pressures of working a job you don't believe in can ravage your sanity and wreak havoc on your entire life.

- *Factotum*—About absolute job-detachment—how to go from job to job and not worry about it in the slightest.

- *Glengarry Glen Ross*—A set of steak knives. Will you even get that? Probably not.

- *Haiku Tunnel*—A hilarious study of procrastination and of what can happen when the weight of all the

work that's not getting done reaches its breaking point. After you see the movie, ask yourself, "What is my seventeen letters task?"

ORGANIZE A YOGA CLASS

To strengthen your body and mind. To get in touch with yourself. To exert and relax your muscles. To find and share inner peace. And, also, to meet and get to know all the hotties in the office. That's right—you have the perfect opener to go and meet all the well-toned, good-looking people on every floor in your building—to see if they'd be interested in doing yoga once a week.

All you have to do is find a yoga instructor who is willing

to come to your office once a week during the lunch hour for a set fee, utilizing one of the office conference rooms for the class. If you can get around ten to twelve people to commit, it will cost around $10 to $15 per person. Make sure to have everyone pay for ten classes up front, so they do indeed commit to coming. You'll be known around the office as a sophisticated, well-rounded person who cares about both the body and the mind, and your company will most likely support your efforts. Go through the HR Department to get official approval—those folks live for proactive mind/body improvement (or at least sending emails out about it). And if your head of HR is into yoga, you will have no problems whatsoever getting the class sanctioned by the company. She might even find a way for the company to pay for the class.

AVANT-GARDE ELEVATOR SMALL TALK

Office small talk is bad, but elevator small talk is the worst. Trapped in that confined space, the shoulder-to-shoulder or face-to-face closeness, the complete strangers lurking behind and in front of you hearing every empty, ridiculous word out of your mouth.

"How's it goin?" your coworker asks.

"Good, and you?"

"Oh, well, I wish it was Friday!"

"No kidding," you say.

Awkward pause, and then:

"Cold out there . . . I'm not ready for that . . . Burrrrrr."

"I know, I know, supposed to be even colder tomorrow," you reply.

"Really burrrrrrrrrr."

"Tell me about it," you say, thinking to yourself, *But really, please don't!*

Thankfully, you arrive at your floor, and as the elevator doors slowly open (*Man, it takes forever,* you think), you say your quick goodbye and hop off. After the doors close, you physically have to shake off the awkwardness of the small talk.

There's no avoiding these conversational snoozers, but if you've got a theatrically inclined cohort in the office, why not agree with this person to make the elevator a moving improvisational performance space, turning your elevator ride together into more of a theater-of-the-absurd type of situation.

It may go something like this:

"Man, have you ever installed a door on the ceiling . . . Whew. Tough work."

"No, I never have . . . just cabinet doors in dirt . . . Where does your door lead to?"

"Depends on the dream."

"Now, that is a dangerous door. I hope you put a good lock on it."

"Oh yeah, I did. Especially after last time . . ."

"Here's my floor, catch you later."

"See you later—keep that door locked!"

Or something like this:

"When you have spaghetti and meatballs, how many meatballs?"

"You don't know? Everyone knows that."

"We'll how many?"

"I know you know. You're just messing around, right? Everyone—*everyone*—knows how many meatballs."

"Well apparently not, because I don't know."

"Okay, this is my floor—I'm not going to tell you how many meatballs . . . You just think about it. I know you know how many meatballs. You know that you know . . . Just think about it."

ffice pools, contests, and races all serve to break up the monotony of the day-to-day, and perhaps even instill some energy to the work at hand. These things also build up camaraderie among you and your fellow coworkers, so the more people involved, the better. But of course there's always that option to work extra hard (much more effort than you'd actually put into your work-related work) to make sure the guy you hate the most is on the losing end of a contest that puts him in the elevator wearing a football helmet. (See Fantasy Football Smackdown on page 63).

Who Will Be Named "The Lasagna King"? Football players have the Super Bowl, baseball players have the World Series, wrestlers have Wrestlemania, celebrity wannabes have *Survivor*, but what do we regular ol' worker bees have? Nada, zero, zilch. Why do we always have to be the spectator? Shouldn't we, too, have competitive challenges in which we must pour our sweat and tears, all in the name of beating down someone else and getting crowned #1?

That's where the Lasagna Contest comes in. Announce that someone must be named the Lasagna King, and pick a date for all those up to the challenge to bring in their best lasagna—easy to transport, hearty to eat, and flavor options galore. Agree on judges (doing your 110 percent best to stack them in your favor, of course), and invite everyone into the conference room for lunch on the big day. At the end of the meal, there can be only one, and that *one* will hold the title of Lasagna King as far as your office walls extend.

The contest is all in good fun, of course, a way to make a typical boring day stand out a little, a way to extend the lunch hour and, hopefully, make the time at work pass a little faster. But make sure you get the office assholes and biddies involved. Those are the folks you want to, hopefully, serve up a super-size dish of crushing defeat.

Other contest options:

- Best Cookies
- Best Eggnog
- Best Cupcakes
- Best Banana Nut Bread
- Best Salsa

Best Cup of Office Coffee. Why does office coffee leave such a bad taste in your mouth—a taste which, of course, lasts for hours and takes a tooth brushing and five pieces of gum to fully get rid of? No doubt most of it has to do with the cheap-ass coffee your company stocks the pantry with, as well as the old and abused and rarely cleaned machinery. But the human factor cannot be excluded. After all, your coworkers, the same people you regularly witness working at half speed and churning out half-assed work, are the ones making the stuff.

Create a win-win for everyone in the office by holding a Best Cup of Office Coffee Contest. Assign each participant a morning of the week, and on their designated morning, participants are responsible for brewing the coffee—they can bring in their own coffee, or try to work magic with the coffee provided by the company. Offer up a rating system: "Damn good cup of coffee" being the highest rating, "Thanks for the all day bad breath" the lowest. Given that each of their names is tied to a specific morning's pot of coffee, and no one wants to be associated in any way with bad breath, your coworkers will truly be inspired to achieve that "Damn good cup of coffee" level.

Elevator Racing. When you're running late for a meeting, that's when you are guaranteed to be sitting in the elevator bank waiting for forever for an elevator to arrive and open its door. Naturally, it will be full of people, and all the floor numbers will be lit up like a Christmas tree. You spend the time imagining the cables being cut and the elevator free-falling all the way down the shaft.

There's a bit of an adrenaline rush involved there, but it's all negative. That heart beating is less about a thrill and more about the bursting of a coronary. Over what? A meeting? You need to put that energy into something more constructive, like elevator racing.

You can do this with one or more coworkers. Agree to go down to the lobby and back to whatever floor you are on once, twice, or three times. Do it individually, clocking each person's performance—the better the person's luck in terms of fewer floor stops along the way, the faster his or her time will be. The person who has the fastest time wins. The loser buys lunch.

Meetings Pool. Are you at one of those companies that holds meetings on how to have more efficient meetings? At every turn in a project, is a meeting held? Is every other email in your inbox a meeting invite?

You're probably in need of MA—Meetings Anonymous, but of course, that would just be one more meeting to attend.

Well here's one way to help the situation. Organize an office pool in which people guess how many meetings they will have to attend over the course of a month—the person who guesses closest to his actual number of meetings attended is the winner. Hold a meeting at a local bar to celebrate the winner.

A special prize should also go to the poor sucker who has to attend the most meetings over the course of a month.

NOTE: This isn't just about making light of how many meetings you have to attend. This isn't just about boosting morale among your overly meetinged cohorts. This exercise also serves to identify which managers and higher-ups hold the most meetings, which in turn reveals who the least decisive, most ineffective leaders are at your company—the ones who will be slowest to act, make the wimpiest moves (the complete opposite of bold moves), and will always play it safe. Make sure to toast these overly paid saps a few times during your meeting at the nearby bar.

Fantasy Football Smackdown. Of course you're already playing, and spending time each week managing your team. My God, if you put as much effort into your work as you do considering all the variables and strategies and odds in your fantasy football league, you'd be promoted to senior vice president in no time.

With that in mind, it's imperative that you "care to make it interesting." Yes, I'm talking about an office pool, and yes, I'm talking about betting real money. But the stakes must be put higher. Money means winner takes all—only one person benefits. There should be something of the "priceless" variety that can be shared by all. In order to achieve this, the last place finisher has to pay in a way that hurts more than thinning his wallet. He's got to make a jackass out of himself.

Some suggestions:

- He has to wear a football helmet to work.
- He has to ride the elevator all through his lunch break wearing the helmet.
- He has to bring everyone a plate of piping hot chicken wings to his or her desk for lunch wearing orange shorts and a Hooters T-shirt.
- He has to wear the jersey of his least favorite team.
- He has to decorate his cubicle/office with the paraphernalia of the team he hates the most.

The Most Emails in a Day Contest. It is absurd how many emails one gets in the course of a day. One hundred emails before lunch is not unusual. If you go on vacation for a week, you can come back to thousands of unread messages. Add in the spam, and the number goes up exponentially. The efficiency of instant communication has created a hulking and unstoppable monster of inefficiency.

Put together a competition to see who gets the most emails in a day (or week). It doesn't really matter who wins—the winner could either get free drinks at the nearby pub or a booby prize. The more interesting thing will be you all revealing how many emails you get each day. Though the ridiculousness of the numbers will just confirm what everybody already knows—that we all get too many emails—the individual tabulations, not to mention the collective number, will still blow everyone away. If only you got a dime for every email you received. You'd be rich, and your wealth would grow very, very quickly.

OPTION: Run the contest over several weeks or a month, with each day's results posted on a public whiteboard. At the end of a designated time period, add up all the numbers—the totals will be like space shuttle mileage or, pushing it further into the stratosphere, as high as the salary of your company's CEO.

Back from Vacation Pool. It's always awful when a coworker returns from an extended vacation. She's so tan and relaxed and happy, it's like she's been replaced by a more joyful and well-balanced version of the coworker you once knew as haggard and angry and disgruntled. Alas, the upgrade is temporary. It doesn't last. We all know this from our own personal experiences. Just like that perfect tan, the glow of refreshment and *Isn't life just grand?* attitude fades. Fast.

But how fast? An hour? A day? A week? It's all up in the air—and that's why it's the perfect opportunity to place bets. That's right, another office pool. On what day will the old version of your coworker return—who looks like she not only never went on vacation, but really, really needs one, even though she probably hasn't even unpacked her suitcase from her very recent trip.

CHAPTER FIVE

Surreptitious Projects

Y ou certainly can't speak your mind out in the open or broadcast your true feelings about the workplace, or even work in general—that's a surefire way to be labeled as a "negative, disgruntled employee" and get yourself fired. And yet, it's so unhealthy to keep it all bottled up inside. A positive, solid, long-lasting relationship requires open and honest communication. That's where the following surreptitious projects come in—they allow your voice to be heard, even if you are the only one who knows that it is you that is doing the communicating. Under the cover of an empty office, hallway, or common area, there is incredible opportunity to reveal some cold, hard truth about work in general, or your workplace specifically. Plus, there's nothing like a little subversive activity to help you feel like you're pulling one over on the man, as opposed to the more common status of the man pulling yet another one over you.

OPTION: If it's easy to borrow a video recording device

from the A/V Department, or if you have your own digital video recorder, try to capture reactions to your projects with a hidden camera. Edit the video into a little show: *The Truth About Work Revealed,* or *[Name of your company]'s Funniest Office Surveillance.*

IMPORTANT NOTE: Don't put any type of recording device in a bathroom. That'll not only get you fired, but arrested and put in jail as well.

VERY IMPORTANT NOTE: These projects won't be very surreptitious if your entire office is wired with surveillance cameras. Don't *you* get caught on tape.

Truth in Muffins. Set out a tray of muffins or donuts or bagels. Then, put a sign in front of the tray that says, "For Upper Management Only."

You Are Being Watched. Hang signs in the bathroom and in the office kitchen that say, in big bold letters, "Now Under 24-Hour Surveillance."

Making Hard, Long Looks in the Mirror Harder. Tape a sign to the mirror in the bathroom that reads, "Is this what you wanted to be when you grew up?" Other suggestions:

- "Bored?"
- "Objects in mirror appear more tired than they actually are."

- "Wipe that smirk off your face."
- "Welcome to your worst nightmare, sunshine!"
- "Yes, you are going bald. And you really do look that fat."
- "Better-looking people go farther."

Vending Machine Messaging. Tape a sign on the vending machine that says, "Don't do it, fatso." Or "Please stock with those little bottles of Jack Daniel's."

Memorial. Tape a flower to an inconspicuous wall and leave a note that says: "Jim just couldn't take it anymore. He made a running start and slammed himself into this very wall. He never woke up. We like to think he's in a better place now."

Candy Voting. Put out two bowls of M&M's, one bowl filled with red M&M's, the other bowl filled with green M&M's. In front of the red M&M's, put a sign that says, "I am working hard." In front of the green M&M's, put a sign that says, "I am hardly working." See which bowl of M&M's is emptier at the end of the day.

WORKING FOR THE MAN
RULE #73 • If you are told to take the lunch order for a group meeting, your instinct will be to feel like a pathetic loser. And though you are clearly low man on the totem pole, you now have a great deal of power. Simply isolate the people you dislike, and make sure to fuck up those particular people's orders: If they don't want mayonnaise—hello mayonnaise. If they don't want mustard—hello extra mustard. If they don't want cheese—extra cheese please. You are not a pathetic loser. You control the most important thing about that meeting—the lunch. Use your power wisely. And vindictively.

Other signs to put in front of the M&M's:

- "Not" and "Exactly"
- "Red pill" and "Green pill"
- "Happy" and "Other"

Lost Snake. Hang a sign up in the common areas that says:

$1,000 REWARD*!
LOST SNAKE!
While we were away at our sales conference in Cabo
San Lucas, our pet snake escaped. It feels like a part of
us is missing! Please help us find our snake! Call
anyone in Sales if you have a sighting. He doesn't bite!
He is not poisonous! He's really
lovable! He's a part of our team
and we really miss him!

**WORKING FOR THE MAN
RULE #74 •** Bonus if the one
person you down-deep hate is
the only vegetarian attending
the meeting. Make sure you
order a tray of the meatiest
sandwiches available. For the
chips, specify that you only
want bags of those deep-fried
pork rinds.

Avante Garde Cake. Make a
cake. A big one. Write something
obscure on the top of it. Ideas:

- "Granulation Ration"
- "Brainstorm Sugar Burger!"
- "WorkerBot Incentive Device
#237"

*The reward figure should be high—so high that people will wonder how it is
that Sales has so much money to throw around for a reward . . . not to mention that "sales conference" in Cabo.

- "Here's to the End of the Meeting"
- "Congratulations Fired Employee #7,536"
- "Yes to Junk Mail"
- "Complaint Box Casserole"
- "Let's Get Forwarding"
- "Cubicle 404, YES!"

Then, place the cake in your office's kitchen area or break room. Put paper plates and plastic forks next to it, and make sure to cut out a slice, so people know that it's okay to eat. Don't let anybody see you bring in the cake.

Moving Art Gallery. Create some bad art and frame it. At the bottom of the frame place a small but official-looking note—with the company logo—that says "Featured Employee Art." Buy some of those hooks that attach to the wall

> **WORKING FOR THE MAN**
> **RULE #75** • One way to take it upon yourself to boost company morale is to post a picture of a sinking ship, emblazoned with the company logo, all around the office.

through suction, and then hang the art in the elevator. See how much art you can hang in the elevator before the jig is up.

Management Notes. Put notes up all over the office that simply read ". . . —The Management." In other words, management is saying *something*, but what it's saying is absolutely nothing, which is pretty much exactly right.

The Wanted Poster. Bring in your digital camera, and snap some pictures of a particular coworker. Do your best to capture an image in which he seems a little off—either angry, or exhausted, or best of all, looking goofy. Then, blow up the picture to eight-by-ten, make photocopies of it, and put the copies everywhere—on the stall doors in the bathroom, on the bulletin board in the break room, on people's desks, even slipping copies into files and into the pages of books on the community shelves. The perfect time to do this is on a coworker's birthday—that is, it can be your gift to a coworker that you despise. But because you've put these copies *everywhere*, it's the surprise gift that just keeps on giving.

Premature Congratulations. Place a big cake in the break room that says "Good Luck [name of coworker]—We'll miss you!" Don't be the one to tell your coworker about the cake—no doubt some gossipy sucker will do the work for you: "I didn't know today was your last day . . . ? Congratulations!" Your coworker will go from totally confused to totally freaked out in a matter of seconds. Make sure you ask for a slab of her goodbye cake.

From a Concerned Coworker. Start leaving notes around the office from "A Concerned Coworker." Have the notes go progressively from reasonable (yet slightly annoying) to totally insane:

- "The inside of the microwave is absolutely disgusting! Is

WORKING FOR THE MAN RULE #76 • After management issues a stern warning and vows to find the person responsible for the illegal acts of vandalism on company property (note that it does not deny the truth of the picture), you can boost morale further by Photoshopping images of management in sailor caps into the picture of the sinking ship, and post even more copies all over the office and even out in front of the building.

this how you behave in your kitchen at home? I don't think so. Please keep the microwave clean. If you make a mess, clean it up!"— A Concerned Coworker

WORKING FOR THE MAN

RULE #77 • If someone makes a PowerPoint presentation with the word "factoid" running throughout it, see if you can get on his computer and do a quick search-and-replace on the file, changing every instance of "factoid" to "null and void."

- "Let's make sure we all recycle paper and print out draft copies on already-used scratch paper. Do not waste! It's about the trees, people, the trees!"—A Concerned Coworker

- "We all have to use this restroom. Common courtesy is a must! This is not just about being professional— it's about hygiene. This is a serious health matter, so let's all be respectful and not leave a mess in OUR restroom."—A Concerned Coworker

- "Please stop leaving food out, even if it's wrapped and stored in your desk drawers. I am starting to see bugs. Sometimes my desk is completely covered in giant roaches. They seem to appear and then hide in the blink of an eye."—A Concerned Coworker

- "Some of us are trying to work! Please keep all your whispering and hateful, spiteful, vindictive comments to yourself!"—A Concerned Coworker

- "I do not appreciate the narrowing of the hallway. Please do not continue to shrink the space between these two walls!"—A Concerned Coworker

- "We must stop the evil forces! Now more than ever—MORE THAN EVER—we must work together! Together! TOGETHER!"—A Concerned Coworker

Office Blog (by Anonymous). Ah, good ol' Anonymous. The things he or she can say! The vitriol. The biting humor. The payback. The revelations. The gossip he or she can spill. And of course, since you are anonymous, you get to have all the pleasure in dishing out and giving up the goods.

How much more fun work can be knowing that via the World Wide Web you can expose all the BS to the world: the absurd, pathetic, ridiculous things that go on in your workplace. Careen right along the edge by not quite naming full names, but be dead-on descriptive about the things that actually happen. How freeing it will be to get it outside of your disgruntled head.

Be sure to inject yourself in there, in a very negative light, to throw off those who are trying to expose who this troublemaking Anonymous is, and if your blog gets big enough, that will be pretty much everyone in your office. Do not tell anyone, even your most trusted coworkers, that you are the one writing the blog. Someone always tells someone, and eventually, you get busted. But if you keep it all to yourself, you'll most likely be able to remain, as your byline reads, Anonymous.

Leave Your Bookmark. Create an outrageous bookmark for the lame "business" books that are found on every executive's shelves and surreptitiously slip it into the books.

Some suggested ideas for the bookmark:

- "As if you're really going to read this book."
- "As if you really read this book."
- "As if you are going to actually implement the ideas put forth in this book."
- "My 'original' ideas came straight from this book."
- "This jackass gave me this book: _____"
- "For Bookshelf Only. Not to Be Read."
- "I fell asleep right here."
- "The CEO that dictated this book to a ghostwriter left the company in disgrace."
- "I didn't get past this page."
- "Hot Fad to Total Fade."
- "Leaders Lead. Followers Read."
- "The author of this book is currently awaiting trial for fraud."

Celebrate Secretary's Day. On Secretary's Day, get a discounted bundle of Happy Secretary's Day cards from the office supply store, as well as some bulk chocolate, or perhaps some lollipops. Then, fill out the cards with a simple, to-the-point message: "Thanks for all your hard work and all that you do for us—We couldn't do it without you. Happy Secretary's Day!" Place the chocolates or lollipops in the envelopes with the cards and seal them up. Then, place the cards on desks of high-level people.

SEX AT WORK
Offices can be such a dreary place. But if you walk the halls in search of nooks and crannies to get intimate with someone,

well, that sheds a whole new light on the place. Make a point of viewing the office not as a drab, lifeless prison, but as a sexual playground. You are thinking about sex all day long anyway, so why not put it in context—the very specific context that is your office. Treat it as a work project with a due date. Remember, you give 110 percent.

Of course you want your experience to be spontaneous, but that does not preclude the importance of being prepared and truly understanding the lay of the office landscape. Hence, a rating system. Note that sex is, in general, a five-star thrill, so thrill levels all begin at five stars. Ten stars is the highest rating.

Restraint level: how loud you cannot be

- *Low:* Let it all out: the heavy breathing, the shrieks, the oh my Gods, the yes, yes, YESes!, the early warning orgasm alerts, the nasty talk with smacks.
- *Medium:* Muffled heavy breathing (using that firm but pleasurable covering of the mouth), the occasional cry of sheer ecstasy, the big finish, but don't assume no one is around.
- *High:* Pretend like if you make a sound, the killer will know exactly where to find you.

Chances of getting caught ratings defined

- *Minimal:* Maybe the cleaning crew will walk in on you.
- *Medium:* Most likely your encounter will be recorded by the office security camera, and possibly witnessed by the security guard. (Do regular searches on YouTube.com to see if your encounter has made you an Internet porn star!)
- *High:* People in the office may see you (1) naked, (2) having sex, and (3) will tell everyone about it by the next day.
- *Extreme:* Your boss may catch you and fire you and will enjoy the fact that the circumstances of your termination were more humiliating than usual.

Now that you understand the ratings, here is a compilation of suggested places at your workplace to *do it*. This list is far from complete, but it's a good start, and will certainly inspire your creative juices to flow that dirty mind of yours into coming up with all manner of twisted and tight spaces to *get busy*.

Your office: Too easy, but of course, it has to be done. Shut the door and go for it. Maybe keep the shades open to add a little extra to the thrill. A nice memory for later, when you're sitting at your desk, alone, late at night, working on something utterly endless and horrible, wondering what it's all for.

Upside: You can get completely naked, go for as long as you like, and know that your boss and coworkers are just beyond the walls toiling away while you're getting laid.

Downside: Just like the bedroom, it may become old hat after a while.

Chances of getting caught: minimal
Restraint level: low
Thrill level: ******

Your cube: Sort of like having sex in a wide-open field. Of course, instead of flowers and long grass flowing in the wind, it's fluorescent lights, computers, and phone cords—but you're having sex, so suddenly all that dreary blandness fades away and it's a glorious, vibrant, star-filled night. At least until you orgasm.

Upside: You'll see your cube in a whole new light.

Downside: Very little cover. Have to wait until everyone has left the office, which means you'll have to stay at the office pretty late.

Chances of getting caught: high
Restraint level: high

Thrill level: ********

In the bathroom: Perfect for a nooner, but the bathroom is pretty much free and clear for rendezvous anytime—morning, noon, and night. Make it a challenge by doing it at all three intervals in one day.

Upside: Sexy dirty.

Downside: Could be just plain dirty. And worse, it may stink.

Chances of getting caught: minimal
Restraint level: medium
Thrill level: ******

Storage room: Make it really sexy by sending a text message: "U. Come fuk me. In strg rm on 13 nr elvtr . . . Rt NOW!"

Upside: Nice, tight, and dark.

Downside: Smell of bleach, or musty boxes, or paper products, or a combination of all three.

Chances of getting caught: minimal
Restraint level: medium
Thrill level: ******

On the copy machine: Get creative. Add a little art to your sex by documenting the experience. See it as a scrapbooking exercise, or a photography-like session.

Upside: Titillating keepsake.

Downside: The documentation may (1) fall into the wrong hands or (2) be a glaring reminder that you need to lose a few pounds.

Chances of getting caught: medium
Restraint level: high
Thrill level: *******

In the stairwells: The thrill of public sex with a nice intruder warning system—doors opened and footsteps in stairwells boom loudly and echo nicely. Of course, most people are too lazy to use the stairs, so you'll most likely be free and clear to fuck, fuck, fuck.

Upside: You'll sort of feel like an international spy having a super secret rendezvous with a dangerous paramour.

Downside: Not everyone wears the kind of shoes that will alert you to an approach.

A little of both: Just like footsteps and opening doors, your moans and groans will boom loudly and echo nicely. Will either enhance the moment or get you caught.

Chances of getting caught: medium
Restraint level: medium
Thrill level: ********

In the car in the parking garage / lot: If you're a cheater, this is the place for you. Very little chance of getting caught, by coworkers or your significant other.

Upside: Memories of the steamed-up car window make-out sessions of your youth.

Downside: Smell of urine, screeching tires, cramped space. And it will be suffocatingly hot in the summertime.

Chances of getting caught: minimal
Restraint level: low
Thrill level: ******

In the elevator: A challenge. Dare yourselves not to hit the emergency stop button.

Upside: Nothing like a moving, frenzied quickie.

Downside: That elevator could stop at any floor, and

those elevator doors may open up quicker than your quickie.

Chances of getting caught: extreme

Restraint level: low

Thrill level: *********

The conference room: A meeting you won't mind attending. Do some "blue sky" brainstorming on positions. No idea is too out there.

Upside: There's a lot of table to work with.

Downside: A particularly revealing "presentation" if you are caught.

Chances of getting caught: high

Restraint level: high

Thrill level: *********

Your boss's office: Perfect place to role-play. If you're in the boss's office, that means somebody is the boss, right? Time to make some crazy, unreasonable demands.

Upside: Nothing says fuck you to the boss more than fucking in his office.

Downside: If caught, your departure from the company will be guaranteed, and it will be more humiliating than the usual firing.

Chances of getting caught: medium

Restraint level: high

Thrill level: **********

During those moments of extreme boredom—say, in a play that your significant other has bought expensive tickets for and forced you to go to—there is something that you can do to save yourself: You can fall asleep. You might have to face the fury of said significant other later that night, but at least you made it through that play without completely losing your mind, or shouting, "Hurry it up already" during the middle of what seems like a never-ending second act.

Unfortunately, you don't have the luxury to go into that safe, comfortable zone of sleep during a meeting at the office. But the good news is that there are safe, simple and even fun methods of meeting survival that can help you get through even the lamest of PowerPoint presentations.

to-do list

MEETING SURVIVAL TECHNIQUES

Conduct hold your breath contests. Challenge a coworker to the contest before the meeting begins, coming up with simple hand signals to reveal when to start. Make sure to sit across the table from each other, so that you can stare each other down while at the same time acting like you're very much engaged in whatever is being discussed. Just trying to keep your composure, not to mention a straight face, will make the meeting much more entertaining.

Pass notes. You mastered this back in Latin class during your high school days, going back and forth with a piece of paper, writing the meanest things you could think of about people who were sitting right next to you. Even back

**WORKING FOR THE MAN
RULE #78** • The second you sit down at your desk with some takeout that (1) you've really been looking forward to eating and (2) cost you more than you usually allow yourself to spend on lunch, you will be called into an emergency meeting.

then it was childish and wrong, but remember, this is about survival: The nastier the note, the more engaged you will be.

WORKING FOR THE MAN
RULE #79 • The calling of an "emergency" meeting is really just an announcement that somebody fucked up big-time.

Go over your to-do list. Whether it's your work list or personal list or both, make it look like you're just taking excellent notes on the meeting.

Send downright dirty text messages to your significant other. See "Sex Messaging" on page 169.

Write some dialogue for your novel or screenplay. If you've got any scenes that involve bogus corporate-speak and blowhard nonsense, you'll have more than enough inspiration flowing throughout the room.

Replay classic movies in your head. Choice selections include: *Rocky III* ("There is no tomorrow! There is no tomorrow!"), *Meatballs* ("It just doesn't matter! It just doesn't matter!"), *Raiders of the Lost Ark* ("Snakes. Why'd it have to be snakes?"), *My Bodyguard* ("You broke my nose!").

Replay confusing movies in your head. Whether it was a movie with some twist that you never really figured out, or a plot that was so convoluted you are not sure whether it made sense or not, or some bizarre ending that left you wondering if you completely missed something, try to sort it out in your head. Some selections: *Oceans 12, Caché, Dead Again, The Prestige, Memento, Mulholland Dr.*

Go around the room and try to decide what kind of underwear everyone is wearing (or not wearing). This is certainly more exciting if (1) there are lots of good-looking people in the room, and (2) those good-looking people are of the sexual gender that you orient toward.

The Proper Name Game. You may or may not remember every one's name in the meeting, even if everyone did the whole business card exchange thing, but decide, based on the person's look, voice, and personality, what name he or she *should* have. Her name might really be Sharon, for example, but to you, due to her high-pitched voice, idiotic ideas, and obnoxious self-importance, she's really a "Gwynnie." Or give everyone an inappropriate but dead-on nickname. Some examples: Lucy, the hot chick wearing all red: Lucifer. Blake, the stud in the nice suit: Steak. The bloated tech guy named Stuart: Sturver.

WORKING FOR THE MAN RULE
#80 • The surest way to get no credit for your original and worthy contributions is to share your best ideas in "brainstorming meetings."

See how fast you can make eye contact with everyone at the table. You'll find that if you stare long enough at a person, you can catch their peripheral vision and draw their eyes right into yours. Consider it a personal experiment on nonverbal human communication. You'll probably find that the people who you get along with will acknowledge your glance right away, but the folks who you don't get along with will do everything in their power to keep from making eye contact with you. In other words, you'll exchange smiles with the people you like, and you'll annoy and make uncomfortable the people you don't. Now that's a meeting that actually serves a worthwhile purpose!

Perfect the art of meditating with your eyes open. Instead of going out of your mind with anger at the fact that you have to just sit there for what seems like forever and listen to a bunch of people you don't like blather on and on and on, take advantage of the time to further your effort to achieve inner peace through meditation. Even if you don't get anywhere close to "inner peace," at the very least it will help

> **WORKING FOR THE MAN**
> **RULE #81** • There is always one higher-up who likes to say—well past the point where the meeting should have ended—"Is there *anything* else? *Anything* else we can be doing? *Any* other ideas?"

you get through the meeting in a calm and peaceful manner, as opposed to finally giving into your frustration by blurting out "JUST SHUT UP! SHUT THE FUCK UP!" and hurling your chair through the window.

Imagine your own all-office broadcasts. It's a good thing they test the emergency broadcast system in your building, because if there ever was a fire or some other type of dire situation, that communication would help save your life. Unfortunately, because they test it all the time, usually when you are on some kind of important conference call or on a tight deadline that requires total concentration, it's mostly annoying and you pretty much ignore it. But imagine if you could gain control of that broadcasting system and make announcements of your own throughout the entire building:

- "It's one-fifteen. Do you know where your employees are?"
- "SEEXXXXXX. SSSSSSEEEEEXXXXXXXX. SEXXX XXXXXXXXXX."
- "Congratulations to Joanie C. and Angela P.—they're both wearing the exact same outfit today!"

- "Attention, attention: IT is monitoring computer activity—All workers currently checking their personal webmail accounts, please immediately report to Human Resources."
- "Welcome to today's meditation moment—where we think about nothing for sixty seconds in order to achieve a sense of calm about how we are all accomplishing nothing of real importance and essentially wasting our lives. Take a deep breath, exhale, and begin."

One thing is for sure, people would start listening to the broadcasts over the system. It might even save lives.

Devise fantastical office projects. While you probably have numerous ideas on how to improve the office, some of them, they're just not possible: that torture device designed specifically for your boss, for example, or your plan to easily convert the office into a sexual dungeon after everyone leaves for the day. Other projects are simply beyond your technical skills, such as being able to shut down—in an untraceable way—your company's computer network at will, or sending out an IM to everyone at the company that says, "THE CEO HAS ALREADY LEFT FOR THE DAY AND HE MAKES 3,000 TIMES WHAT YOU DO (not including stock options)." But it is absolutely, positively therapeutic to let your imagination run wild, and there's no better time to let

> **WORKING FOR THE MAN**
> **RULE #82** • No one says anything, because they desperately want the damn meeting to end.

your mind wander than during an endless meeting. Though you may not get to see your project in action, it's always good to dream, and to dream big at that. You certainly spend enough time daydreaming at the office to come up with countless ideas, but here are a couple fantastical projects to get you started:

- *A wired meeting room*: This room isn't wired to the Internet or as a video conferencing room, but it is wired with sensors that loudly or brightly (or both) indicate idiocy, long-windedness, bad ideas, blowhardedness, and unfunny jokes. The room can indicate these typical meeting room behaviors through flashing sirens, a booming *2001: A Space Odyssey* HAL 9000–style voice, or lit-up "Applause"-style light boards. So, for example, if your boss is doing his obnoxious and useless "I'm just thinking out loud" thing, the sensors would pick up on it and the appropriate indicators would be activated. Obviously, manual control of the indicators would be an option, which would make it even less likely for meetings to drag on forever or for people to act like idiots and blather on with their really bad ideas.

- *Office robots:* Not as extreme as the robots that go haywire at the beginning of *Robocop* (and shoot up all those executives), nor as benign as those robots that deliver prescription drugs in high-tech hospitals, the robots you would create and program for your office would have a temperament and function somewhere in the middle. They won't just be wall-flowers, but they aren't going to go so far as to commit violent murders (at least none that could be traced back to you, anyway). That leaves a great deal of room to work with. Imagine—and that is exactly the goal of this exercise—the tasks you could assign these robots: In your stead a robot could attend meetings with outside salespeople. You could program it to listen intently, ask a few good questions, and then say "No, thanks" in a firm but polite fashion to end the meeting at the appointed time. A robot could deliver insults to people you dislike in a voice and tone of your choosing: (sexy voice) "Just wanted to let you know your ideas are terrible and everyone around the office thinks you are a Class A moron." A robot could sit in on staff meetings, programmed to announce loudly and bluntly when someone has been speaking too long, is repeating herself or saying something someone else has already said, or is making absolutely no sense. A robot could regularly track down and either ogle or roughly grab the ass of the lecherous creep in the office.

MEETING SURVIVAL BINGO

You may have heard of or even played Buzzword Bingo—instead of numbers, the twenty-five bingo card squares are filled with buzzwords. Played during office meetings or seminars or conference presentations, the first person to mark off five in a row, or four corners, or blackout (whatever you establish as "Bingo")—wins.

The bingo card on the following page is a riff on that—but instead of just buzzwords, it includes various things that occur and drive you crazy in meetings.

Obviously, each player's bingo card needs to be unique in terms of the placement of the words/phrases/incidents, so take the sample Meeting Survival Bingo card and randomly apply the twenty-five items in the squares to different positions on as many cards as you need.

OPTION: Change out items in the sample card with things that are specific to your office. For example, if there's a guy in your office who always seems to spill his coffee during meetings, make that one of your twenty-five items.

B	I	N	G	O
1. A coworker dozes off.	6. Someone says, "Verticals."	11. Can't connect to Internet to open presentation.	16. Not enough handouts for everyone.	21. Two people whispering are told to be quiet.
2. Someone is doodling.	7. Someone says, "Next steps."	12. Projection onto big screen does not work.	17. Someone gets testy when he or she is interrupted.	22. Someone apologizes for being sick.
3. Someone says, "Bottom line."	8. Someone walks in late.	13. Can't "conference in" someone on the phone.	18. Birthday surprise cake arrives.	23. Someone complains that the meeting room is freezing or too hot.
4. Someone starts pitch by saying, "Ummmm..."	9. Someone sneezes.	14. Meeting starts late.	19. More than five minutes are spent discussing someone's recent vacation.	24. Person on conference call gets made fun of.
5. Audible yawn.	10. Cell phone goes off.	15. Someone uses a Venn diagram on whiteboard to convey his or her concept.	20. Boss berates entire staff.	25. Someone suggests yet another meeting.

MEMO
handy excuses to get out of meetings

Though you can't get out of *every* meeting, here are some excuses to limit the number that you do have to attend, or lessen the amount of time you have to spend at each one:

- Explain right at the start that you've got another meeting scheduled to begin in just thirty minutes, so you'll have to duck out early.
- Have someone come in and tell you that you've got an important call. Excuse yourself, saying, with a very, very serious face, "I really have to take this one," and then dash out of the room as if you've got a real emergency on your hands.
- Excuse yourself to go to the restroom, and then don't come back until the meeting is just breaking up. When you do reenter the room, make sure to nod your head a lot and shake hands with everyone so it seems like you're really engaged and involved and fully aware of what was going on during the meeting.

the Cubicle

Your cubicle is about the furthest thing from a castle, but in the workplace, it is your home—the place where, like it or not, you spend countless hours. If those walls could talk, well, let's just say it would be lots of complaining and proof of your sorry little corporate existence. Not anything you'd want to hear. But it doesn't have to be that way! Don't just hang a calendar, keep one plant alive, and put the obligatory framed picture of your significant other near or on top of your monitor. Take ownership of your cube, despite its half walls, built-in fluorescent light, plastic windows featuring views of the coworkers on your left and right, and lack of a door.

to-do list

THE MOST PRO-WORKER CUBE

Start an informal contest, and spread the word around the office liberally: The person with the most pro-work cubicle wins.

There is no shortage of slogans and motivational quotes to blanket your cube with, and no shortage of worker-bot accessories to showcase these bumper sticker bits of wisdom on how to live life to the fullest and achieve success in the workplace.

"There Is No 'I' in Team!"

Exactly! Not that anyone is ever truly influenced by these slogans—except for a hard roll of the eyes—but get your pals, or more precisely, your team—to "Embrace the Challenge," "Go for It," "Work Smarter," "Roll with the Punches," and "See It Through."

From posters to coffee mugs to mouse pads to pens to calendars to bumper stickers, there's a real opportunity to cover your entire workspace in the shallow, one-sentence zingers that have about as much impact as the hot air expelled to say them out loud.

What does the winner win? Who decides who wins? Details, details. Keep it very informal or organize like the football or March madness pool.

Bonus: No one can get in trouble with this one. After all, it's all pro-work. What's your boss going to say: "Take down that poster that says 'There's No 'I' in Team!' Get rid of all this positivity right now!"

BECOME THE CRAZY CAT PERSON, LESS THE CATS

There's always that one person in the office that literally has all of her cubicle walls covered in pictures of her cats. Not only that, but they change—holiday-themed photos during the Christmas season, costumed cats around Halloween, cats skulking around Easter eggs around Easter. And of course there are also the requisite cat calendar, cat stuffed animals, cat mousepad, and cat screen saver to really, fully, and totally complete the (scary) picture.

You don't want to copy this person . . . you might not even have a cat. This is about taking the crazy cat person's enthusiastic aesthetic, less the absolute dedication to our furry feline friend the cat.

In other words, you should do something very cool and totally overwhelming with your cube space. Make it the biggest something—whatever it is that you're into: stars, Bollywood, Charles Bukowski, UFOs, Sophia Loren, Dr. Seuss, surfing, Andy Warhol, knitting, Nikola Tesla, fancy hats, expensive boots, clowns. (Definitely do the clown thing if a coworker you particularly don't like has mentioned a fear of clowns.)

BEACH BALL MADNESS

Get to the office early one day and place a brand-new deflated beach ball in everyone's cubicle. Do this in the spring, on one of those perfect days when all your coworkers small talk about how they wish they could be outside, sipping cocktails. It will not be long before beach ball madness ensues in the cubicle ranks. Beach ball madness is when blown-up beach balls are launched into the air and start bouncing all around. Over the cubicle walls they will come, and over the cubicle walls they will go. And once the madness starts, it never really ends. There may be stoppages, of course, long ones, but there will always be a beach ball around, and there will always be that one person who decides to fan the flames of the madness by launching it over a wall.

SELF-PORTRAIT FLIP-OFF

Take a picture of yourself looking annoyed. Then, print it out (or photocopy an enlarged version) so that the picture takes up an entire 8.5-by-11 sheet of paper. Tape the sheet—face in—at the very top of a shared cubicle wall. Why tape it face in? So that when your coworker annoys you by talking too loudly or asking you a ridiculous question for the millionth time, you don't have to say a word; you can simply flip over the sheet of paper, so that your self-portrait is staring right at your coworker. Message sent.

DANGER: Your coworker could very well steal your self-portrait (it is in his cube area, after all), make lots of copies of it, and pass it around the office. Or, your coworker could scan your self-portrait, email it around to a few friends, and inadvertently launch an email campaign that leads to your self-portrait (looking the opposite of your best) going truly viral, quickly zipping its way into the inboxes of bored office workers around the world.

OPTION: Don't use a self-portrait. Use a picture that conveys extreme annoyance (a growling animal, for example) or simply features a curt, direct phrase, such as "Shut Up."

WRAP-A-CUBE

A coworker goes on vacation and spends an entire week lying on some exotic beach, sipping fruity cocktails—and she doesn't think there will be consequences for her while you and others stay stuck in a dreary office doing the same old, same old, asking each other, "Is it Friday yet" all week long? Let her know how much she was despised—in a friendly sort of way—by covering her entire cube, and everything in it, in wrapping paper. To get to work upon her return from paradise she'll have to tear apart paper covering the entryway, the monitor, the keyboard, her pens, her framed pictures, and yes, even the phone. Be sure to take pictures of the entire process—from the wrap job to her reaction at seeing her cube to the tearing up of all that paper.

Other options:

- Fill the cube with packing foam peanuts.
- Turn everything upside down or facing the wrong way—all the books, pads of paper, the calendar, files, the mousepad, the stapler, even the desk chair.
- Cling-wrap everything with that clear plastic wrap. Or use tinfoil.

MEMO

one-way conversations You've overheard coworkers have while they're on the phone

You can decorate your cubicle (or the cubicles of others) to your heart's content, but unfortunately, you cannot soundproof it (them). This means that as happy as you might be to have just the right look and feel to your little nook in the bland corporate landscape, there is no way to shield your ears, from, say, the baby talk your next-door neighbor uses when he talks to his girlfriend. Here are some other samples off the soundtrack of your wall-less, door-less daily grind. All the more reason to put some effort into your cube environment—at least you'll have something nice to look at.

- "Why didn't you call? . . . No . . . No . . . But why didn't you call? No . . . I'm just sick of it. SICK OF IT! I sat around all night, and I was mad, MAD, and then, when it got really late, I started to get worried. Where were you? Why couldn't you have just picked up a phone?! Just make a quick, simple call? . . . No. I'm sick of it, just sick of it. Why didn't you just call? . . ."
- "But my doctor *always* just calls in my prescription. He never faxes anything! He won't. He will call, but he will

not fax. Who uses faxes anymore, anyway? I need that medication. I am totally out. Can my doctor just call, like he always does? This is, like, an emergency."

- "And then his mother called and she wanted to talk to ME! I couldn't believe he even told his mother, but he hands me the phone and I'm like no way, no way, but he just starts pleading with all these weird faces and hand gestures, so I finally get on the line and I am like, 'I am NOT going to speak to you about this!' and she starts crying, and like, begging, and I was like, 'Your son is a grown man . . . ' "

- "What do you mean you didn't mail it? SHIT! I needed those documents. SHIT! Well, you'll just have to overnight it. What? What? No, no, OVERNIGHT IT! Do you understand? I need those documents. SHIT!"

- "Hello, yes, hello? Yes, I ordered a . . . Yeah, okay, I'll hold . . . but for just . . . Hello? Shit. Hello? HELLO? Yes, I ordered a pizza over an hour . . . Hold? No . . . Hello? Yes, I ordered a large pepperoni pizza like an hour and a half ago . . . Hello? Hello? Ahhhh, Shit."

- "Yes, I finished the project report and emailed it to you at 3 p.m. Yes . . . Yes . . . I knew . . . Yes . . . But . . . I understood you needed the report by 2 p.m. . . . Right, but . . . Yes, 3 p.m. is not 2 p.m. . . . So yes, it was an hour late but . . . Right. Okay. No, it will not happen again. I'm sorry the report was late, and it won't happen again."

CHAPTER EIGHT

Documentation

As a bot in the corporate machine, you see and experience some of the most absurd things imaginable, and are witness to human behavior at its most petty. Cooking under the pressure of dissatisfaction, stress, and passive-aggressive maneuvering, all manner of the ridiculous, inappropriate, and outrageous occurs, whether it's a nasty message from a coworker, the office pantry left in disarray, or a nonsensical corporate memo handed down from on high. You wish you could just forget about it all—put everything that happens at work completely out of your mind when you leave the office. But that is not going to happen. So instead of trying to separate yourself from all the workplace shenanigans, embrace them through documentation. Seek out and preserve the culture of your workplace, and share your findings in a humorous way. It may or may not be material for your novel (See Write Your Novel On the Clock on page 159), or your blog or MySpace page, but your documentation projects will make it easier and more fun to mentally process the grating experience of your daily grind.

to-do list

THE WHITEBOARD ALBUM

Jokesters frequently have fun with whiteboards by commenting on or adding words to the very serious whiteboard notes from earlier meetings. Seeing I LOVE LONG MEETINGS!, CODE THIS, BITCH!, or DO NOT ERASE in huge letters that cover an entire, otherwise blank board is enough to make you crack a smile. And though it might be juvenile, seeing the word "blow" before every instance of the word "job" might just make you bust a gut, especially in the context of whiteboard remnants from an important board meeting about how to make the company more competitive.

> **WORKING FOR THE MAN**
> **RULE #83** • The longer it takes you to compile the monthly report, and the thicker it is once it's finally bound up, the less time people will spend actually reading it.

But even without the jokesters, the corporate shorthand left on whiteboards, especially empty and worthless bullet points derived from "brainstorming sessions," can be enough to put you over the edge:

- Build website
- Drive Traffic
- Increase sales
- = More revenue!

So easy it is to erase a whiteboard, all this good humor and insight into the joke of corporate life literally wiped away forever. Unless, of course, you make a point of taking photographs with a digital camera of these whiteboards from time to time, thereby preserving the prankster commentary as well as the ridiculous ramblings of corporate drones working their way through totally forgettable meetings.

Collect these photos into a little booklet and leave it near the eraser on the whiteboard's shelf. No text is necessary to make your point. The jokey one-liners as well as the incomprehensible notes on the whiteboards featured in the photographs will say it all.

THE STINKING SINK

Document the horror that is the sink in the office pantry, which serves as a daily reminder that your coworkers must live like filthy animals/frat boys in their homes. Take a daily photo of the mess your coworkers leave each and every day: the plastic Chinese take-out container that someone intends to reuse but, of course, just like the action items from the last meeting, simply forgets about. The half-filled coffee mugs with spoiled milk clouds. The detritus from a supposedly healthy salad, the oily leaves now blocking the drain and causing a pool of dirty water to fill the sink. Make a photobook out of it, or post the series of images on the cupboard above the sink when you have enough to make your point: Clean your fucking dishes, fuckheads!

WORKING FOR THE MAN RULE #84 • Nobody really cares about the monthly report you compile. Unless you turn it in late. Then people care. They'll act like the world is about to end, sending you urgent emails and leaving you testy voice mail messages, making mental notes about your incompetence and failure to deliver all along the way.

Other common areas of the office to document:

- **The inside of the microwave.** People fire up their various foodstuffs: breakfast burritos or "cheese" pizzas or uncovered bowls of leftover spaghetti. The food either burbles out all over the plate or splatters all over the inside walls. After the ding, they take their food and leave, as if the microwave is a self-cleaning contraption. You might think the microwave is especially dangerous (How does that humming little box heat up food, anyway?), but it's really just a regular ol' hazard of uncleanliness and food filth.

> **WORKING FOR THE MAN**
> **RULE #85** • Your company will issue a ridiculous new policy on April 1. It will be *so* ridiculous that you will think that it must be a joke, because, you know, it's April 1. But it won't be. The policy will be real (confirming once again that your company is a joke pretty much any day of the year).

- **The floor near the door in the bathroom.** People dry their hands with paper towels and then either just totally miss the garbage can (Why are the opening slots always so small?) or use the paper towels as a sort of makeshift glove to open the door (Don't want to make contact with those nasty germs!) and then simply let them fall to the floor. So thoughtful, so sanitary.

- **The conference room.** People bring in muffins and coffee and granola bars, eat and drink during meetings, and then simply leave their garbage after the meeting breaks. Did they see waitstaff taking orders and busboys clearing off the table? Of course they didn't. They're just rude and discourteous.

- **The copy/printer room.** They make their copies or print out documents from their computer, only to mess up or find an error that forces a do-over. Maybe some jerkoff has (yet again) left labels or letterhead in the printer, making the documents unusable. Instead of taking the mess-ups and placing them into the recycle can, they just . . . leave it all there (unless it's their résumé). After a few days of this, not only has a forest been felled, it has all been for nothing but a cluttered mess.

THE TINFOIL PRIZE

The office microwave never seems particularly safe—always the cheapest one off the shelf, always overused, frequently burning popcorn, and always treated abusively. On top of all that, there's always a new tinfoil-zapping moron every few months who, in cooking up his or her leftovers, cooks up some tinfoil, releasing god-knows-what radioactive or poisonous gasses into the office. To celebrate this individual, create a giant tinfoil trophy to be placed upon the jackass's desk. The trophy should be big enough for all to see.

SECONDARY PAYBACK: Remember that scene in *Erin Brockovich* where Julia Roberts serves up water from the polluted water source to the lawyers representing the power company, making her point in the most poignant way possible? What a fantastic idea, a

**WORKING FOR THE MAN
RULE #86** • Not following the rules (such as accounting rules) will get you fired if you are caught, but following the rules will either prevent you from making your numbers, allow someone else to get ahead of you, keep you from getting promoted, or get you fired. It is the crux of working for the man, and remember, we are all working for the man.

variation of which can be used to drive home why it's not cool to carelessly utilize a community microwave.

Give a warmed-up slab of apple pie over to the tinfoil zapper, and after he takes a bite, say, "That was heated up in the microwave where you cooked up that tinfoil." Bonus points if you can capture his facial expression with a camera.

> **WORKING FOR THE MAN**
> **RULE #87** • If you work your ass off and do amazing work, but dress like a slob, the thing that will register in most people's minds when they think of you or hear your name is that you are that guy who dresses like a slob.

NOTE: There is one upside to a tinfoil-in-the-microwave incident: The microwave gets replaced, and you get to use a clean microwave for a day.

EMAIL CHAIN BOOK

Save all the ridiculous email chains that are indicators of (1) the kinds of idiots you work with, (2) proof of how much time people waste at work, (3) how petty people are in the workplace, and (4) how much of what we do all day at work is totally and completely meaningless. Put a "best of" collection together, and circulate it around the office through interoffice mail.

For example . . .

To: Office All
From: Jenny
Subject: A Conservation Idea
Hey everyone—

I don't want to weird anybody out, and this is probably

going to upset some people . . . I don't know, but since our city is facing a serious drought, I thought maybe we could go "Mellow Yellow" in the bathrooms. That just means that we don't flush every single time, because it really helps conserve a lot of water.

> **WORKING FOR THE MAN
> RULE #88** • If you don't do shit and never really accomplish anything, but wear really nice suits to work, the thing that will register in most people's minds when they think of you or hear your name is that you are a sharp dresser and must really be going places.

Feel free to come talk to me about this idea with questions or concerns. I did this back when I lived on the West Coast, during severe drought seasons. If I don't hear from anyone, I'm just going to go ahead and start doing this.

Any thoughts?

———

To: Office All

From: Paolo

RE: Mellow Yellow

I'm down with this. When I was in college, my roommates and I did this to conserve water just as a general rule.

———

To: Office All

From: Elaine

RE: Mellow Yellow

Well, honestly, I could say that I'm up for it here in this email, but I have to admit that if I walked into the bathroom and was actually confronted with the practice of "mellow yellow," I'd probably be pretty grossed out . . .

To: Office All

From: Melissa

RE: Mellow Yellow

Uh . . . Sorry, folks. Maybe I'm just too prissy, but I don't want to walk into a stall unless the toilet has been flushed.

To: Office All

From: Colin

RE: Mellow Yellow

I have an idea: why don't we limit ourselves to drinking water only every three days. My understanding is that the human body can survive, if it has to, on that kind of a regimen. And if we drink less water, we won't have to urinate as much, and therefore we won't have to flush the toilet as often. We'll be doing double duty conservation. Any thoughts?

To: Office All

From: Jenny

RE: Mellow Yellow

Okay, well, it looks like some people aren't really into the idea . . . How about if we designate one stall in each bathroom as the Mellow Yellow stall. That way, people who are interested in conserving water can use the designated stalls, and those who need a fresh bowl can use the other stalls? Sound good?

WORKING FOR THE MAN RULE #89 • The colored dress shirt topped off with a white collar says, "I am not sexy, period."

To: Office All
From: John
RE: Mellow Yellow

Why don't we all piss in a bucket, and not use the toilets at all. And since Jenny and some others are so worried about water conservation, they can drink from the bucket! Sound good?

To: Office All
From: Vanessa
RE: Mellow Yellow

Alright, that's it. I am sick of people using Office All about these kinds of issues. I don't care if you've lost your keys, or you found a scarf in the conference room, or you want to know who ate your food from the fridge. And I certainly don't want to see a discussion about Mellow Yellow. I've got work to do and I assume all of you do as well. So let's get to work!

> **WORKING FOR THE MAN RULE #90** • The sneaker commute look—a skirt, jacket, and panty hose with sneaker footwear—is one of the unsexiest looks possible.

VOICE MAIL TIME CAPSULE

Save all your voice mails—not through the voice mail system, but on a totally separate recorder, preferably something digital, so that you can easily edit a greatest hits collection. Such a collection would most likely include all those angry, unprofessional diatribes, as well as those long, rambling, ridiculous calls about nothing from that spacehead who is *always* leaving messages like that.

Why do this? Because ten years from now, most of these coworkers will totally fade from memory—you won't just forget their names, you'll forget about them completely. And you'll certainly have no recollection about whatever important matters they are leaving messages about. Listening to these workplace voices of the past, and having no idea who the voices belong to or what they are talking about, says a great deal about the workplace. You spent five days a week, eight to ten hours or more each day, working with those people at that place, and yet, you can't remember who the hell that person is leaving you an urgent, panicky message about some important document that she needs right away, or else! This audio blast from the past will serve as an excellent way to remind you that in the scheme of things, the day-to-day of your workplace experience—even the people you work with in close quarters hour after hour, day after day, week after week—is not something that registers in a deep and meaningful way. All that stress, the politics and backstabbing, the unprofessional dickhead, the office hottie, the projects completed and the reports turned in on time—it all just fades from memory (except the hottie—you never forget the hottie and his or her own very special brand of hotness).

THE JOY OF AN ANGRY VOICE MAIL MESSAGE
If you get an angry, unprofessional message from someone, a message that borders on being downright threatening, don't

get upset. Don't pick up the phone and return the favor with an angry message of your own. Don't go down to the asshole's office and give him a piece of your mind. Certainly don't tell him you're going to kick his ass. Don't get mad at all.

Instead, save the message on a digital recorder. Then, go do some research. Chances are good that you are not alone in getting a message like that from this particular person. Your task is to determine who also has received such messages, and who might have them saved on their voice mail system or possibly on some other kind of recording device.

Be proactive as well. Talk to the people who have to work for, under, and with this guy, and explain how you received a really terrible, inappropriate voice mail from him, and that you have it saved. Play the message for those to whom it makes sense—people you already have a relationship with. Then, encourage these people to save any future angry, threatening messages they may get from this person, and to alert you.

The goal is to collect as many of these unprofessional messages as possible. Put them on a CD, and then deliver it to Human Resources, the guy's boss, directly to the perpetrator, or to all three. No one likes a bully. Bullies often get away with their transgressions, especially if they're top earners. But mounting evidence cannot be ignored. Your target might not get fired, but you won't be getting any more angry voice mails.

PROOF THAT ZOMBIES EXIST

Start bringing your camera to work. Go around to your coworkers, ask each of them to pose like a zombie, and snap a picture. The key is not to do this project all in one day—spread it out over time. Don't let your coworkers know you are photographing everyone in the office. A picture of one of your coworkers pretending to be a zombie is sort of funny—but a collection of *everyone* in the office in their various zombie poses—now that really is funny. Post the pictures early one morning in a place where everyone in the company will stumble upon them.

Other types of poses:

- **Sleeping:** To reveal the true level of enthusiasm in the office.
- **Angry Face:** Tell them to imagine that the boss has just handed back their work and that they have to stay late to make a "few changes."
- **Tired:** Shoot your photos either right when people arrive at the office or at the very end of the day.
- **Too Happy/Delirious:** Instead of "Cheese" have them say "I love my job!"
- **Bored:** Should be easy for everyone to handle this one. Could also be described as "Candid."

CAPTURE PURE HAPPINESS ON FILM

Take a picture of a coworker on her last day on the job just as she is shutting down her computer and about to walk out of her office or cubicle for the very last time. The caption: "My single most favorite moment during my long tenure at [name of company]."

And don't forget to take a self-portrait of yourself on your last day of work. You won't necessarily be all smiles. If you didn't handle your two weeks' notice period right, you'll be stressed out and exhausted from having to get last-minute projects done, doing last-minute training sessions, and attending last-minute meetings with coworkers, managers, and your boss to go over all the work you are thankfully leaving behind. You're totally replaceable—everyone is—but that doesn't mean you didn't have some relevant work in the hopper, some useful contributions that can be squeezed out of you that will be helpful to others after you've left for good. The picture will reveal all. It will be easy for you to tell whether you're smiling for real or just trying really hard to curve your lips in an upward direction.

CLIENT IS JUST A FANCIER WORD FOR CUSTOMER

While coworkers are certainly the people you have the most interaction with at work on a day-to-day basis, your customers are right up there in terms of being able to make you want to hurl your computer at the wall and hide under your desk. Perhaps you refer to your customers as "clients," but the word "client" is just a fancier way of saying customer. You may be managing a million-dollar account, but that won't prevent your customer from yelling at you like you forgot to put large fries in his take-out order. There's no way around it—when you have customers, you are in the customer service business, and you get treated as such. And you are at your customer's mercy. Do or say the wrong thing, and you will be fired. As an employee, you are an expense. A customer is revenue, and revenue always wins out. That is why the customer is always right.

In other words, you will have interactions with your

customers that will drive you nuts. That is, until you start documenting them. They are so absurd that you could not make the stuff up. Write it all down, and use the bits where it makes sense to—in your novel, screenplay, blog, or that one-sheet that you share with trusted coworkers. You may find the dialogue so original that instead of getting annoyed when you are engaged in a hostile conversation with a customer, you will be happy to have some more fuel for your creative endeavors. At the very least, you'll find the process therapeutic—hashing it out on paper and revealing the ridiculously brazen words being thrown your way will get it out of your system, instead of echoing around an ache-filled head.

MEMO

various conversations between a designer and some of his "clients"

"Well, since my name starts with an M, what I was thinking for the logo was doing the Golden Arches thing."

"You mean the *M* from McDonald's?"

"Right. The Golden Arches. I really like that look."

"Well, the thing is, that's a trademark, and McDonald's takes that stuff pretty seriously. And I like the Golden Arches, but it's probably not the best idea . . ."

"How about if instead of using the color yellow, we used the color blue . . . Would it be okay then?"

"All right, I want like every word to blink, but at different times."

"What do you mean, every word?"

"Well, not every word, but every important word."

"I don't think anyone will be able to read the text on your website. It will be really distracting."

"I thought about that. But it will be so cool-looking, and sort of like a game. I just know it will make people want to really check out the site."

"Can you fit these pictures of my dog into the design somehow?"

"Well, we've already spent a lot of time implementing the concept we discussed last week, and I'm not really sure how a picture of a dog will fit in . . ."

"No, not just one picture. Pictures . . . Look—I'm not even a professional photographer or anything—but these photos just came out really amazing. So I really want to include them in the design."

"Why did it take you six hours to do this basic design?"

"Well, we had to type in all the text, remember?"

"Yes, I do. But I mean, how long did it take you to type in those pages? How many words a minute can you type?"

"I was thinking you could put like a wrestling spin on the design concept."

"Wrestling?"

"Yeah, you know, like the professional wrestling television shows."

"Well, but your store sells office supplies, right?"

"Yeah, but wrestling is really big right now. I mean, wrestling is where it's at."

more documenting rules

WORKING FOR THE MAN RULE #91 • The office hallway is not only a path to the restroom or the elevator bank. It also serves as a training ground for the "half-smile"—the fake smile that you flash and then immediately drop as you pass by coworkers. The skill with which you handle this facial maneuver is acquired over time, and true talent is revealed in your ability to drop your smile the millisecond you are out of eye contact, perfectly gauging the unique range of each person's peripheral vision.

WORKING FOR THE MAN RULE #92 • Once you are a manager of more than fifty people, you don't have to worry about the hallway half-smile anymore. You can just avoid eye contact altogether or, if you feel like it, stare people down with a really mean scowl. People might think it's personal, but you're just being honest about how you really feel inside—you're on the clock just like everyone else.

WORKING FOR THE MAN RULE #93 • There are always certain people in the office that don't bother playing the hallway half-smile game. They just don't smile, ever.

WORKING FOR THE MAN RULE #94 • The women in HR are constantly trying to make their hallway half-smiles better, hiring consultants and attending seminars to reach their full potential.

WORKING FOR THE MAN RULE #95 • If the hallway half-smile was an Olympic competition, members of the sales force would be the gold medal contenders. They have to work it, of course, but mostly it's just a God-given talent.

WORKING FOR THE MAN RULE #96 • There will be one person at your office that has brought in a blender (To mix some kind of energy/muscle-building drink? Faddish diet formula? Margaritas on the sly?) and will leave the pitcher portion in the sink. It will be left there—taking up lots of room—for days, the liquid left inside eventually turning into a stinking, swampish swill.

WORKING FOR THE MAN RULE #97 • It is okay to take that blender (if you dare touch the pitcher while it's in the sink) and throw it in the garbage without remorse.

WORKING FOR THE MAN RULE #98 • As soon as you send out a note reminding everyone about a no-exception policy, the VP of Sales will make a decision to make an exception to the policy—"Just this one time."

WORKING FOR THE MAN RULE #99 • "Just this one time" really means "Anytime we feel like it" to the sales team.

WORKING FOR THE MAN RULE #100 • An exception to a no-exception policy will be made if money is on the line.

WORKING FOR THE MAN RULE #101 • It does not take a lot of money to make an exception to a no-exception policy.

WORKING FOR THE MAN RULE #102 • Policies that guide ethics and good practices only exist to use as defense exhibits in lawsuits.

WORKING FOR THE MAN RULE #103 • Revenue generation—however and from whoever; no ifs, ands, or buts—generates the true policies.

WORKING FOR THE MAN RULE #104 • Revenue generation often requires that ethics and good practices be thrown out the window.

WORKING FOR THE MAN RULE #105 • It does not even really need to be revenue in the sense of actual dollars—as long as it can be booked into the revenue column.

rom the day before Thanksgiving all the way
through New Year's Day, nobody is really work-
ing. Oh sure, we all show up at our offices, sit at our desks,
and go through the motions of getting our work done, but really, we're taking in the holidays—buying gifts, sending out
holiday cards, making travel plans, getting ready to welcome
guests, going to holiday parties, and overall just getting
caught up in the holiday spirit. Work is the last thing on our
minds.

Thanksgiving is the perfect warm-up. After all, that's just
a big meal and lots of traffic. Christmas and New Year's are
gifts and parties and holiday cards, not to mention that whole
holiday spirit thing. People are just plain nicer around the
holidays, and that includes people in the workplace.

Now is not the time to take your sick days. This is actually a really good time to be going to the office. The reality is,
you've got lots of personal stuff to take care of, and the best
time to get that stuff done is while you're getting paid for it.
Besides, the more time you spend taking care of all the details of the holiday season while you're on the clock, the

greater the amount of holiday cheer you can take on after hours.

to-do list

CHRISTMAS/HANUKKAH/FESTIVUS/KWANZAA CELEBRATORY PREP, POMP, AND CHEER

Here's a compendium of things you can do on company time in between all the conversations with your coworkers about eggnog recipes, the Charlie Brown Christmas special, upcoming trips home, the office holiday bash, end-of-the-year bonuses, and of course, all the holiday parties you've been invited to attend in your dressed-to-the-nines, kiss-me-under-the-mistletoe best:

Make your holiday cards. I'm a major proponent of people making their own holiday cards. It's so easy to make a really cool card—just get some nice card stock paper, preferably something right out of your company's copy room, and write a short poem or greeting. Then, with good double-stick tape, preferably from your company's supply room, put a picture of whatever (you and your family, you and your dog—you and whoever, looking happy and cheerful, essentially) on the front. Voilà! You've got yourself a card.

Address your holiday cards. The real pain in the ass is addressing all those envelopes, unless of

> **WORKING FOR THE MAN RULE #106** • If you want to take down the morale boost that is the office holiday party, spread a rumor that no alcohol will be served.

course you're one of those annoying types who have mailing labels for your friends and family. But addressing envelopes on company time isn't so bad, and it actually creates the impression that you are working. Hop to it. You don't want to be one of those schmucks whose Christmas cards arrive on January 3.

Get your shopping done. Forget the long lines on the weekends. Take a long coffee break and hit the stores. Or of course you can do it all online.

Plan your holiday party. You should not only make your invite list, but also get in touch with everyone on it. Do your shopping for the party while you're on the clock as well. About the only thing you won't be able to do is prepare the food.

> **WORKING FOR THE MAN**
> **RULE #107** • If you want to further take down the morale, spread a rumor that all the higher-ups already had their office holiday party at the swankiest restaurant in town, and that they were all encouraged to bring their spouses.

Plan menus. Hell, try something new. Search all the cooking websites and dig up some really cool recipes.

Hoard vendor gifts. You know which of your vendors had a good year (and are possibly charging too much) and which ones had a lean year by the gifts they send during the holidays. Of course, start-ups flush with cash always send the most ridiculous gift baskets—the more ridiculous the basket, the more likely the company will be out of business before the end of Q2 in the new year. Regardless, even the lower-end stuff coming into the office is usually worth grabbing up—fruit baskets, cookies, fudge, boxes of chocolates, and more. It's usually a free-for-all (yes, in the spirit of the season, even gifts addressed directly to you should be put out for all), so watch the space where this stuff gets put out like a hawk.

Get some holiday party booze. Run some of the extra bottles out of the office and into your home. The holiday office party is usually early on in the month of December, so this helps you stock up for your own holiday gathering, as well as all the parties you'll be attending until the end of the year.

Avoid the long lines at the post office. Ship all your packages and cards using the company mail. All the supplies are there—and not just boxes and packing tape. You should be able to find regular tape and wrapping paper around the office as well, allowing you to take care of the whole wrap, package, ship process in one fell swoop.

Try to figure out what you're doing on New Year's Eve. This is always such a bitch. Total stress. First, you're worried that you won't get invited to any parties at all. Then you're trying to figure out who is going where. Then you have to try to make it so that you can be in five places at once. Start planning now.

Make holiday calls. Auntie Margaret and Uncle Joe would love to hear from you, so give them a call. On your company's dime, of course, which also means you're actually earning while you hear about cousin Suzy's first year at college and explaining why you didn't make it to Florida for a visit this past year.

OF COURSE IT'S NOT ALL ABOUT YOU

'Tis the season for giving, after all. The holidays offer up all kinds of inspiration for projects and activities that you can participate in with or perpetrate on your coworkers. They can be of the nice or naughty variety, but in the end, it should all be in good fun. Except for those folks who really do deserve coal in their stockings. For them, it's okay to go the full-on, 100 percent naughty (nonsexual) route.

Secret Santa. This is an office standard. Usually you draw a name out of a hat and the only rule is the dollar amount you are allowed to spend. Sometimes gifts are exchanged at a conference room gathering, and sometimes that involves a game where you can go around the room and steal or trade gifts from everyone who participated. All good office fun, and yet, similar to that regularly scheduled birthday cake gathering, it's a little stuffy and slightly uncomfortable, like extended elevator small talk, but with gifts.

Options to mix it up a little:

- Do the drawing of the names and put a fixed amount on the money each person can spend, but add the stipulation that whatever you receive, you have to keep in your office or cubicle for all to see for an entire year. Obviously, you can't buy anything gratuitous or clearly against office policy, but if you're the Secret Santa of a New York Yankees fan, well, a Boston Red Sox mouse pad might just be the perfect gift.
- More of a fantasy project, but perhaps a true Secret Santa: Buy some cheap stockings from one of those 99 cent stores, and some generic charcoal from your local grocery. Stuff the charcoal into the stockings and hang on the doors of all the executives. Or just your boss. Or the coworkers you despise.

Christmas Tree Decor. Don't ask—just plop a Christmas tree down on your floor somewhere and quickly dash off an email to your coworkers asking them to stop by and, using office supplies or whatever they have handy in their desks, decorate the tree—paper clips, decorated Post-its, a tree skirt made of mouse pads. Send a separate email to the newer employees, people who weren't at the company last holiday season, and impress upon them how this is a beloved, longtime tradition that *everyone* in the office participates in.

If you've got access to employee photos (perhaps the ones on ID badges, available in the company directory), print them out, gluestick them to red or green card-stock paper, and use bent paper clips to hang them in the tree. Another option is to go around the office with a digital camera and take pictures of everyone, print out the pictures on the color printer, and make ornaments out of those images.

Before HR or management figures out what has happened, you'll have taken the dreary knickknacks and trinkets of office life and turned them into agents of holiday cheer. The decorated tree will be somewhat of an eyesore, but no higher-up will be able to mess with it, or will dare order that it be removed. No one will want to be labeled the office Scrooge, the guy who stole Christmas.

Of course, if that does happen, if someone does order that the tree be taken down, make sure that person gets exactly that label.

Office Christmas Caroling. Get a portable CD player and put in an album featuring Christmas songs. Set the volume to high. Place the player—along with a purposefully tacky sign that says, "Happy Holidays from Management"—in front of or very close to a coworker's cubicle/office. Then, press play on the player and quickly walk away. Your coworker will eventually get up out of his chair to see what the heck is going on, at which point he'll see the sign and wonder if it's a coworker's joke or the joke of yet another pathetic attempt by management to boost morale and spread some holiday cheer during the Christmas season.

Holiday Party Rumor Mill. The word is, no bonuses this year, and of course, there's not a single definite word on when you'll get to leave on Christmas Eve.

It's so frustrating not having any information that you might as well start talking as if you actually do know a thing or two about what's going on around the office. So take a break from ordering gifts from online retailers, planning your holiday meals, and mailing out your holiday cards, and seize control of the rumor mill. Instead of just hearing things, contribute to the flow of misinformation.

Be sure to plant your "credibly sourced info" with known office gadabouts—those coworkers about whom people often ask, "What exactly does so and so actually *do*?" These are the people who wander around from cube to cube all day, holding papers in their hands (not for show, really, but more because they're dilettantes and too scatterbrained to actually get the papers to where they're supposed to go), chatting and whispering and essentially wiling away the hours until it's quitting time. These are your misinformation agents. When they stop by your cube, whisper these (sweet nothings to these gossip mongers) juicy bits of disinfo:

- There's not going to be any alcohol at the office holiday party.
- There might be beer and wine, but you have to pay for liquor.
- You can't bring a guest.
- The holiday party is going to be held in the basement.
- The food isn't going to be free.
- The holiday party is going to be potluck.
- There isn't going to be any food.
- The executives and other selected employees already

had a holiday party the other night at an expensive restaurant.

- Only top management got bonuses.
- Bonuses were already distributed in early November.
- If you did not get a bonus, it means that you are marked for termination before December 31, in order to meet the goal of getting rid of "deadweight" and underperforming personnel before the start of the new year.
- Only managers get to leave early on Christmas Eve.
- No one is going to get to leave early on Christmas Eve.

New Year's Resolution Project. On the day after New Year's Day, while everyone is still hungover and not quite gung ho about the start of a new year, possibly feeling quite miserable that they are back at the same job they promised to be rid of last year, have everyone write down New Year's resolutions and put them in a sealed envelope. Explain that they only get their envelopes back when they leave their jobs or at the end of the year—whichever comes first. Though you can't know for sure, it's safe to assume that most people's resolutions will have to do with finding a new job.

MEMO

some reasons why your new year's resolution should be <u>to quit your job</u>

- You just hate getting up in the morning during the work week.
- On Saturday mornings, your first thought is to start dreading Monday.
- The one time your boss said "Good job" last year was right after you had spilled coffee all over your desk.
- You can't remember the last time you actually cared whether or not you did a good job on a work assignment.
- You've started to enjoy talks with the company's cheery publicist, because she seems so happy.
- The senior vice president of your department is still introducing herself every time she sees you, even though you've worked at the company for over a year.
- You realize that even surfing the net, making personal phone calls, taking really long lunches, and going to get coffee two or three times a day still does not make the workday go by any faster.
- You find yourself saying "Whoever thought we'd end up with a job like this" after every conversation around the office.
- When you actually tried to sit down and write that novel you always wanted to write, nothing came to you.

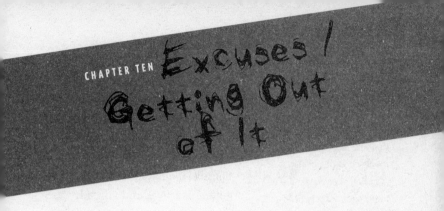

ometimes you just can't get out of bed. Going from total warmth and comfort to the clank and crank of workaday hell is no easy feat, so it's no wonder that there are times that you show up late, or don't make it in at all. The real wonder is how often you actually do show up, day after day, knowing what you are going to have to face.

But for those days that you do opt to linger in bed or just totally blow off the entire day, it's imperative that you have at your disposal solid, well-thought-out, and seasonally relevant excuses. Know the risks and be strategic about usage. And most important, take advantage of the time you are giving yourself outside of the office.

to-do list

EXCUSES FOR TARDINESS

There's nothing worse than feeling that panic as you race your way to work knowing full well that unless you are

**WORKING FOR THE MAN
RULE #108** • If you show up late to work and find yourself standing next to your boss in the elevator, do not start rambling about late trains or traffic jams. Just say hello and either talk about the weather or start telling him how innovative and exciting you think one of his pet projects is.

suddenly endowed with superhero powers, there is no way in hell that you are going to get to the office on time. You feel agitated, and you are sweaty, and damnit, the day hasn't even really gotten started, and already you just want to pull out your hair and scream, and maybe punch out that guy next to you just because he's, like, standing there and breathing, or just ram your car right into the back end of the car in front of yours because . . . It's . . . Just . . . Not . . . Moving . . . Fast . . . Enough. Well, there's no reason to get so hot and bothered. Sure, you're going to show up late, but a good excuse is all you need to smooth over the situation. Instead of freaking out about being tardy, ease your mind and relaxingly focus on coming up with a valid reason for why you didn't get to work on time. Obviously, you can't show up late every day, but on the days that you do, just keep your head on straight and conjure the perfect excuse.

Here are some ideas to inspire your own unique excuses:

- "I cut myself really bad, and I was trying to stop the bleeding. It just wouldn't stop."
  Keys to success: Do not look too upset, as it's just a cut, not a broken arm. Make sure to wear a Band-Aid.

Downfall: You have to wear a Band-Aid religiously (don't let it fall off in the bathroom) for at least a week.

Added benefit: You can type a little slower this week, due to your injury.

• "My cat got out and I had to look for him."

Key to success: Look like you care more about your cat than you do about most of the human race. Cat owners are very serious about their cats.

Downfall: If your boss has never owned an animal or if he hates animals, he might not be sympathetic to your pet situation.

• "My dog got into a fight and was really worked up and scared. I wanted to make sure he was okay."

Key to success: Same as above, replacing the word cat with dog.

Downfall: Same as above.

• "I've got a terrible rash."

Key to success: Your boss will worry that it's contagious and not want you to come in for fear of catching whatever you have.

Downfall: When you come in with no visible symptoms, your boss and coworkers might assume you have some kind of rash in the genital region.

• "There was a power outage and my alarm clock didn't go off this morning."

Key to success: There was a major rainstorm the night before.

Downfall: You see your boss over the weekend in

the neighborhood and realize you both live on the same block.

- "I've got a possible bedbug infestation, and I'm waiting for the exterminator."

  Key to success: Your boss will be skeeved out by the idea of you coming in, and will be more than happy to have you stay at home and deal with your bedbug issue.

  Downfall: Not even the people you like at work will want to come near you, and certainly won't ever want to go to your house.

- "My place was robbed and I had to wait around for the police to file a report."

  Key to success: Your boss will feel genuine concern for your loss and safety.

  Downfall: She asks to take a look at the police report.

- "I hate taking the bus. The damn bus was running late, really late, so that's why I'm late."

  Key to success: Seem highly agitated.

  Downfall: Your boss sees you get dropped off by your roommate.

- "There were major train problems this morning. I don't know if it derailed or what, but I was waiting at the train station for a really long time."

  Key to success: Talk about writing a letter to the mayor complaining about the train system.

  Downfall: Brown-noser who has it in for you later casually mentions to the boss that he had no problems this morning with the train.

- "I don't feel comfortable saying what happened—It's very personal . . . Please just trust me that it's a valid excuse."

  Key to success: Your boss will give you the benefit of the doubt and cut you some slack for being late.

  Downfall: She'll start to wonder about your honesty, and scrutinize the things you say you are going to do much more carefully.

- "My best friend called and he really needed to talk to me. He's having major problems."

  Key to success: You must take your boss aside and "confide" in him your reason for being late. A true friend wouldn't just blurt out someone else's misery for just anyone to hear.

  Downfall: You might not be able to muster appropriate sincerity, given that you were out with all your close friends the night before and they're all doing just great.

- "My car broke down."

  Key to success: Wear a white shirt and put some grease on it.

  Downfall: Your boss saw you parking your car around the corner from the office.

- "My fight club was raided last night."

  Key to success: Your boss will secretly respect your tough-guy lifestyle.

  Downfall: You will be egged on by coworkers at some work-related event to get into a physical fight, and will be knocked out after one half punch.

SUMMER DAYS ARE HERE AGAIN: EXCUSES TO GET YOU POOLSIDE

Summertime means beautiful, warm weather—several months full of wonderful blue sky, swim-trunks and bikini kind of days, the number of which will surely be far greater than Saturdays, Sundays, and two weeks' worth of vacation. Indeed, to sit throughout the summer, day after day, at a desk in an office filled with cold, conditioned air—not unlike the kind we're forced to breathe in airplanes—is just plain wrong.

That's why it's so important to have a good number of excuses to get out of work during these glorious summer months. Following are some excuse options that use the very elements of summer to help you get some more time hanging out poolside, getting a tan, swimming at the beach, or whatever floats your boat in the heat of these sizzling summer days. Use them wisely, so that you don't have to be in the office. Or in pants, or shoes, or clothes altogether, for that matter.

Here are the excuses:

- "It was so hot yesterday that the wool suit I was wearing gave me this horrible rash. I don't think I can make it into the office. My face and neck are just covered with this rash, and my legs as well. I think I'd really scare people, and it's just itchy as all hell . . ."

  Key to success: Redness on the face, administered by your significant other with a few smacks.

Downfall: You unfortunately piss off your significant other just before needing the smacks administered, and she lays it on just a little too thick. Black-eye thick.

- "I fell asleep in the sun yesterday, and I've got a really bad sunburn. I can barely move, and I think I might have to go to the doctor."

  Key to success: You actually have to spend some time in the sun and get a little burned.

  Downfall: You do indeed end up with a very painful sunburn!

- "My air conditioner must have blown out a fuse, and so my alarm clock didn't go off this morning. And it got so stuffy in my apartment that it must have made me really oversleep. I can't believe it's almost noon . . . and I'm just totally dehydrated and not feeling too well. I don't think I'll be able to come in at all today."

  Key to success: Use a gravelly dry throat when you call in and talk to your boss.

  Downfall: Unseasonably cool breezes widely reported on the news.

- "I was doing volunteer community cleanup work in the sun all day yesterday, and I worked myself so hard that I think I'm suffering from heatstroke. I'm not feeling well, so I better stay home today, just to make sure I'm okay."

  Key to success: You have a history of volunteering, especially with charitable organizations that regularly partner with your company on events and corporate-sponsored programs.

Downfall: Your boss spied you lying in the park drinking cold beers from a cooler all day long.

- "I was swimming in the ocean yesterday, and I accidentally swallowed a whole bunch of saltwater, and I'm not feeling too well today. Real queasy. I'm sure it's nothing, but I better stay home, drink lots of water, and rest up. I'm sure I'll be fine by tomorrow."

  Key to success: You look tan, but instead of that relaxed "I spent the day at the beach" vibe, you convey an "I got food poisoning" demeanor.

  Downfall: Your boss overhears you tell a coworker you didn't even get in the water, you just laid out all day.

- "My cat usually goes outside during the day while I'm at work, but right after I let him out, I realized how hot it was outside, and I just knew he should not be out in heat like this. I'll come in as soon as I can, but I've got to find my cat. He just took off. I can't find him. He's a really furry cat and I just know he won't do well in this heat. I'm so worried. I better get off the phone so I can keep looking for him."

  Key to success: Sound completely out of your mind, like your whole world is coming apart.

  Downfall: Your boss finds out that you don't even own a cat.

- "I was rushing to get to work and I jumped into the car and the car seat was so hot that I burned the back of my legs. They're all red and swollen and sore, so I think I'm going to have to let them heal today. It's no big deal—I just wouldn't be able to sit at my desk all day. But I'll be in tomorrow."

Key to success: Wear loose-fitting pants and walk slowly when you do get back to work.

Downfall: Your boss sees you in a spinning class at the gym.

- "I was walking around barefoot yesterday and I stepped on a nail. I could barely walk yesterday, and today it's just a little bit better. I should be fine by tomorrow, but today, well, it still kind of hurts, and I also have to go to the doctor to get a tetanus shot."

  Key to success: Ask a question about tetanus shots, such as "How often are you supposed to get a tetanus shot?" or "Do tetanus shots hurt?"

  Downfall: You are in such a good mood from your day off that your boss witnesses you merrily skipping into the office.

DAYLIGHT SAVINGS EXCUSE

Twice a year, you can show up on the Monday after Daylight Savings begins and ends and, no matter what, just say you got confused about what time it really was, and that's why you are late.

Preface everything with "I don't know what happened" and do a lot of fiddling with your watch, because if you get caught in the logic of a bad excuse, you might be told by your supervisor that technically, based on what you are saying, you should have arrived an hour early, not an hour late. Daylight savings is tricky like that.

Basically, you want to avoid a conversation like this:

"Sorry I was late. I forgot to change my alarm clock."

"Well, that should mean you would have arrived to work early."

"Oh, yeah, I mean, I thought it was fall forward . . . not fall back . . . So I just totally messed up."

"Okay, but if you thought it was fall forward, then you would have arrived to work two hours early. We set our clocks back an hour. We gained an hour this weekend . . ."

"Ummmm, well, yeah . . . No, what I mean is, I . . . I just don't know what I did exactly—I'm really confused . . . I guess that's what I mean . . ."

Remember—keep your answers vague and simple. Don't get specific. If you try to explain it, you'll screw up and get yourself caught in a lie.

WINTER IS HERE, BUT DON'T DESPAIR: FREEZING WEATHER AND RAINY DAYS BRING WITH THEM A WHOLE HOST OF GLORIOUS SICK DAY EXCUSES

When winter hits, just hopping into bed at night can be dangerous: Cold feet become like weapons, sending your own legs running for cover, and the person you share your bed with screaming, "Jesus, will ya put on some freak'n socks!" But it's the hopping out of bed at the crack of dawn that's the real challenge. It's like your body has weights strapped to every limb, and the only message your brain is sending is *Cold. Freezing. Freezing cold. Do not get out of bed. Cold. Ice cold freezing. Stay in bed. Stay in bed. Stay in bed . . .*

There is, however, an upside to the treacherous wintry weather: It provides a wonderland of excuses as to why you can't show up to work, thereby giving you the pleasure of staying wrapped up in the warmth of your down comforter all day long. Nothing beats the season of frost, fog, snow, and freezing rain in terms of the number of ways to get out of work.

So here are just some of the excuses you can use once that winter chill grips the air.

- "I was skiing and I lost my sunglasses after a really serious fall, and unfortunately over the course of the rest of the day I overexposed my eyes to the dangerous reflection of the sun on the white snow, which has temporarily diminished my vision—the whole snow blindness thing. I don't want to risk any further exposure to light and permanently damage my retinas, so I better stay home."

  Key to success: Shield your eyes, even though you are wearing sunglasses.

  Downfall: Your boss throws an orange at you, and you reveal your hand-eye coordination to be working just fine.

- "I had to wash my one and only winter coat because I slipped and fell hard, very hard, last night on a mud-slicked sidewalk, and unfortunately my dryer broke down before the jacket actually got dry."

  Key to success: You have a jacket with a stain that you can wear.

Downfall: For weeks on end, you have to wear that jacket with the stain, and *only* that jacket with the stain.

- "My layover flight has been canceled due to bad weather, and so I'm stuck in Houston, Texas." (You don't want to pick a fun place to be stuck in—such as Miami or San Francisco or New York—so Houston, Texas, is perfect).

  Key to success: Have someone vocalize fake muffled boarding announcements while you are making your call.

  Downfall: Your boss sees you in town.

- "The heat isn't working in my apartment, so I have to stay at home to wait for the repairman. I really hope he comes soon, but apparently he's gotten tons of calls."

  Key to success: Sound really agitated, and say that this guy is worse than waiting for the cable guy.

  Downfall: You boss says he has the same problem, and wants the name and number of your repair guy.

- "I can't make it out of my building because snow is totally blocking the exits. It's just totally piled up so high. We're like trapped in here."

  Key to success: The snow just keeps on falling.

  Downfall: Your boss tells you that snow in front of your door is nothing a shovel can't solve, and that you should be thinking less of yourself and more about the little old ladies in your building.

- "I can't make it out because a storm drain is blocked

and there is a gushing river of rainwater rushing past the exit of my building."

Key to success: Record-breaking downpour.

Downfall: Your boss asks, in a very peeved way, whether you've got any rubber boots.

- "I was rushing to get to work and I slipped on a patch of ice and hurt my back. I was totally, totally rushing, and I think that's why I fell."

  Key to success: Walk slowly and with your hand on the small of your back. Every time you sit down, wince.

  Downfall: You bump into your boss on your nightly run.

- "Rainwater and mud are starting to seep into my house, and I need to sandbag the perimeter. I can't stay on the phone for even another second, 'cause oh my God that mud is a comin'."

  Key to success: News reports of mudslides and runs on sandbags at local hardware stores.

  Downfall: Light rain, rainbows, and clearing skies.

- "My car is blocked in by snow, and it's also flooded—the engine won't turn . . . It just won't start."

  Key to success: Significant snowfall the night before your call.

  Downfall: Your boss knows you have a garage.

- "I've got it all: sniffling, sneezing, coughing, achy, stuffy head, fever . . . I'm hoping the chicken soup heating up on the stove will make me feel better."

Key to success: When you call, sound so sick that your boss actually worries that your germs might be able to come through the phone.

Downfall: Your boss sees you downing shots at happy hour later that evening.

CHAPTER ELEVEN

Sick Day Calendar

here are a lot of workdays in a calendar year, and you only get two official weeks of paid vacation. But those are not the only days you have to seize to hit the beach, lounge around in your pajamas, or extend a weekend and still get paid. You probably have up to ten sick days to do with what you please.

So just like you plan ahead and work out all the details for that trip to Italy, with the same care and forethought you should take a look at your calendar and figure out the best times to take your sick days. For God's sake—on days that you're actually sick, and you aren't going to do anything but moan and groan and watch *Oprah*, get your ass into the office! Don't waste a sick day when you're actually feeling under the weather! Those limited number of paid sick days are to be cherished and fully taken advantage of just like those golden vacation days.

to-do list

PLANNED SICK DAYS

Following is a list of all the holidays (from New Year's Day to Christmas), as well as things like birthdays, anniversaries, and other personally relevant events that can be extended or notched up another level by using a sick day to maximize the fun.

New Year's Day: January 1. Consider calling in sick on January 2. Of course this means using up a sick day at the very beginning of the year, but the alternative is kicking off the brand-spanking-new year pissed off and disgruntled (more so than usual) and possibly still a little drunk. So take that extra day off so that you can start the new year out right.

> **WORKING FOR THE MAN**
> **RULE #109** • A quick way to get through the day is to show up late, take a long lunch, and leave early.

Martin Luther King Jr. Day: Observed on the third Monday in January. Call in sick on either the Friday before or the Tuesday after and make it a four-day weekend. Let freedom ring, indeed.

Valentine's Day: February 14. It goes without saying that you should make your romantically extravagant plans on company time. The key is to work on Valentine's Day, but to call in sick on February 15. That way, you can stay up all night, sleep in late, and then stay in bed *all* day long to recover from and then relive the multiple ecstasies of the night before.

President's Day: Observed on the third Monday in February. Call in sick on the Tuesday after to stretch the three-day weekend into a very presidential four-day break.

> **WORKING FOR THE MAN**
> **RULE #110** • The quickest way to get through the day is to not show up to work at all.

St. Patrick's Day: March 17. If you like to party on St. Patrick's Day, then do yourself the solid of calling in sick on the day after—to give yourself the lucky luxury of recovering from your night of reverie on the comfort of your own couch.

Easter: A Sunday, between March 22 and April 25—it really moves around, so be sure to give your calendar a hard look so you know exactly when it is. Call in sick on the Monday after, due to the family gathering Easter festivities that took place on Sunday (and all the traffic you had to deal with on the way home).

Secretary's Day: Wednesday during the last full week in April. Say thanks to yourself by taking the day off.

Memorial Day: The last Monday in May. Take off the Friday before or the Tuesday after the holiday to make it a memorable four-day weekend.

June: No office holidays in June, but a really great month to take some sick days, given that it's the start of summer and the weather outside is absolutely perfect.

Independence Day: July 4. Call in sick on the day after, which will give you extra time to hit the road and make the most out of your celebratory boozing. Now that's worthy of setting off some serious fireworks.

August: No office holidays in August, but all the higher-ups are on vacation, so you can take "sick days" without actually using up any official sick days. Important month to stay very healthy.

Labor Day: The first Monday in September. You've worked hard all year, so consider calling in sick on the Tuesday after to give yourself a four-day weekend. Technically, this is the weekend to really stick it to your boss. That's what Labor Day is all about, right?

WORKING FOR THE MAN
RULE #111 • The longer you prepare and the more elaborate your phony story is to get out of work, the less your boss will believe your excuse for not being able to make it into the office.

Boss's Day: October 16 (yes, this is a real "Day," featured on many calendars, and with Happy Boss's Day cards to boot). There is simply no better way to celebrate Boss's Day than to call in sick. In fact, to show up on the day that the boss is commemorated is not just totally absurd—it's an insult to every worker out there. October 16 is a day in which you most definitely, absolutely, wholeheartedly must call in sick. Henceforth, October 16 will be known as National Sick Day Day.

Halloween: October 31. Wear your costume to work—it'll be a major distraction, and no one, including you, will get any work done. It's all in the name of teamwork and morale boosting. Carry on the Halloween spirit into the evening (get scary drunk). Then, call in sick on November 1, as a reward to yourself for being such a fun, good-natured employee and gregarious, fun-loving person in general.

Thanksgiving: The fourth Thursday in November. Call in sick on the Wednesday before or the Monday after to give yourself a five-day weekend (given that most offices are closed on Friday). Use the extra time to make even more dishes and consume even greater amounts of food and wine.

Christmas: December 25. Go ahead and give this special gift to yourself—call in sick the day after Christmas. It is the season of giving, after all (and it's one way—just one—to make up for the bonus you didn't get).

Other days to plan sick days around:

- Your birthday
- Your significant other's birthday
- Your child's birthday/Your childrens' birthdays
- Your anniversary
- The day after Mother's Day/Father's Day

Holidays/observances that are not normally recognized with days off in the workplace for which you might want to utilize a sick day (on or around the holiday/observance):

- Ramadan
- Rosh Hashanah
- Columbus Day (second Monday in October)
- Veterans Day (November 11)
- Yom Kippur
- Hanukkah
- Kwanzaa (December 26–January 1)

Events or celebrations that might warrant the use of a sick day or two, depending on your specific tastes and interests:

- Academy Awards (You may not have been invited to the hot-ticket LA after parties, but that doesn't mean you didn't attend or throw an Oscar party with friends, and therefore need a day to recuperate from your excessive, Hollywood-style hard-partying evening.)

> **WORKING FOR THE MAN**
> **RULE #113** • All it takes is one quick call from the office to ruin a day off.

- Mardi Gras
- March Madness
- U.S. Open
- World Series
- World Cup
- Super Bowl
- Day new major video game releases
- If George Lucas makes *Star Wars, Episode VII*

NOTES:

- Be sure to find out how many sick days you have each calendar year, and plan accordingly.
- Make sure you know exactly how many sick days you have at any given time.
- Holidays that fall on a Tuesday or Thursday present an option for a four-day weekend. Just call in sick on either Monday or Friday, respectively.

AN UNPLANNED SICK DAY

Of course there are those days when you wake up and just feel like death—not because you've got a fever and stuffed-up head, but because you are just totally and completely sick of work. The papers are stacked high, your boss is screaming at you for things big and small, all your coworkers are needing you for this and that, projects aren't going right, nor are they getting done on time, and even though you are working your ass off and doing the best you can, you have the distinct feeling that everybody thinks you are a screw-up that can't get anything done right.

The cure for a day like this—when all you feel is the weight of all that is wrong with your job—is to call in sick. Fuck it all.

But you don't want to waste this day—preciously free of time in the office—by just sitting around in your underwear wallowing about all your woes to the morning show talking heads, perking up every once in a while as you begin to buy into those infomercials about making money by purchasing and selling real estate with no money down!

Though you can't know when that perfect storm of work BS is going to lay you out, you can plan ahead for the taking of an unplanned sick day. Keep a checklist of all those things you'd like to do around town (a "staycation")—

**WORKING FOR THE MAN
RULE #114** • Giving out your cell phone number on your outgoing voice mail message or your out-of-office email auto-reply guarantees that you will get that call.

WORKING FOR THE MAN
RULE #115 • You are not showing how dedicated you are when you give out your cell phone number on your outgoing voice mail message or your out-of-office email auto-reply. On the contrary, you are revealing that you are (1) stupid and (2) have no life.

whether it's getting to a museum or seeing a matinee movie or taking a walking tour of a cemetery. Do your research for these types of outings while you're on the clock, of course.

Ideas:

- Local museums
- Drink at the oldest pub in the city
- Shopping!
- Driving range/golf course/new golf shop
- Long run/bike ride in the park
- Spa day/massage
- Antiquarian bookshops
- Farmer's market
- Historical society
- Movie theater that shows old films/take in a matinee

MEMO
a sick day gone awry

Ring, ring, ring . . .

"Hello, this is Michael. I can't make it to the phone right now. Please leave a message after the beep."

BEEEEEEEEP

"Mike, yeah, this is Steve. Betty told me you called in sick today. I hope you're feeling okay. But listen, I can't seem to find the file on the Stevenson account. Please give me a call and let me know where I can find it. Thanks."

Ring, ring, ring . . .

"Hello, this is Michael. I can't make it to the phone right now. Please leave a message after the beep."

BEEEEEEEEP

"Mike, hey, listen, Mr. Stevenson called, and he said he never got that package you were supposed to overnight him three days ago. Ummmm . . . Give me a call so we can find out what's going on."

Ring, ring, ring . . .

"Hello, this is Michael. I can't make it to the phone right now. Please leave a message after the beep."

BEEEEEEEEP

"Mikey, yo, did you forgot about that focus group meeting? You should have let us know. Now we've got all these people, people we're *paying money*, just sitting here. You can't just ignore stuff like this. The team members are *pissed off.* No one knew you weren't coming in today. Just because you're sick doesn't mean you can blow everything off, buddy boy. Give me a call ASAP. People are really *pissed.*"

Ring, ring, ring . . .

"Hello, this is Michael. I can't make it to the phone right now. Please leave a message after the beep."

BEEEEEEEEP

"Mike, Mr. Stevenson just called and said he's heading over to our office right now. He's threatening to take his business elsewhere. Wake up. HELLO. ARE YOU THERE? Come on, Mike. This is serious. Answer the damn phone. We need you here like right now."

CHAPTER TWELVE

Making the Best of the Day-to-Day

ftentimes, the work you have to do while you are on the job is worse than dirty—it's mind-numbingly boring, pointless to the finest point possible, involves dealing with people you don't particularly like and would not choose to spend time with in your life outside the office, and is directed and overseen by morons with extremely poor people skills. Worst of all, this work that you have to put so much effort into is, in the long run, completely and totally meaningless and therefore absolutely worthless.

This leads to feelings of burnout, hate, anger, and despair. You certainly don't feel like working hard, and are disgruntled about having to work at all. Good happy hours with free chicken wings help ease the pain momentarily, but over the long haul, you just get a bigger bulge in your gut and a deeper sense of dread in your core.

That is why it is so important to work hard on the right things, and to constantly look for simple but effective ways to push back and avoid altogether the dreary day-to-day. The right things will be different for each person, but in general,

WORKING FOR THE MAN RULE #116 • The day you wear your brand-new white shirt to work is the day you pick a paper cup—for your morning coffee—that leaks.

they will involve projects and ideas that help further *you* along and allow *you* to benefit from the amount of time you spend in the office. In other words, they help make the job work for you.

to-do list

WHILING AWAY THE HOURS (YOUR LIFE) FOR THE MAN

Calculate the hours you spend at work each week—and be sure to factor in all the time it takes to get to and from the office. Run this number up against the number of hours in a week, less the number of hours you sleep. Extrapolate this information so that you can see the details on a monthly, yearly, and lifetime basis. Assume you will be forced into retirement around age fifty-seven or so, and then will start working part-time (but really just under full-time, so that the company does not have to give you any benefits) until you kick the bucket.

Chart the figures into a PowerPoint presentation. Title it "My Working Life." You will conclude that you spend a great deal of time at work—more than at anything else you do in life, including spending time with your family. So you can't just think of it as all the *time* you spend at work, but rather how much of your *life* you spend at work.

In order to deal with these shocking, depressing figures,

take immediate action to salvage some of your time on this planet—leave the office and go do something that will make you feel like you're taking advantage of this whole life thing, and not just whiling it away in a drab office pushing paper.

WRITE YOUR NOVEL ON THE CLOCK

This is an age-old, time-honored tradition: Writing a novel on the man's dollar. Yes, you can burn the midnight oil, or work on weekends, or take a few months off to pound out your tome, but there is nothing better than writing the words to that novel that may or may not become a bestseller and make you rich and famous while you're supposed to be on the job. The lower-level the job, the worse your boss is, the more depraved the conditions, the better your words, or at least the story of how your words came to the page, will be.

Plus, it should be noted that if you're writing while on the job, you are technically being paid, albeit in a roundabout, subversive way, for writing! That is no small feat. You are probably making more money off of your writing than most published authors. Still, it's not so easy to get writing done while you're on the clock: There are all those urgent emails that pour into your inbox, urgent calls that light up your phone, and urgent requests from your boss to handle the various urgent issues that pop

WORKING FOR THE MAN RULE #117 • The day you wear your brand-new, expensive white pants, someone will spill coffee on you.

up throughout the day. (Why is it that in life, "urgent" means someone is in the hospital, but in the workplace, "urgent" ranges from "Meeting time changed" to "Need that report by EOD"?)

Here then, are some ways to write your novel while you're on the clock:

- Show up early and pound out some writing before the start of your day. Technically you're not on the clock, but it's a great habit to get into, especially if you have a truly demanding job where it's hard to sneak in personal creative endeavors. Wait! Keep reading! Sacrilege, I know, to suggest that you show up early to work. But this really is an excellent way to get some writing done without interruption.

> **WORKING FOR THE MAN**
> **RULE #118** • The day you wear your scruffy jeans and a T-shirt is the day you find out you have to make a last-minute presentation to the higher-ups.

- Or, when you do show up for work, right on time (or the usual few minutes after the official start of your working day), instead of checking your voice mail and email, and then surfing the news and gossip sites, commit to focusing completely on your writing for a solid half hour. You're fresh, and have yet to get sucked into or distracted by all the work-related crapola.
  NOTE: There is no better way to start the day than with a personal creative effort—it will juice you up, get your mind rolling, and instill energy that will

help carry you through the day. If something crappy does happen during the workday (and doesn't something crappy always happen?), the stage you set in the morning will help you work through the negativity.

- Just like you block off time for meetings and various work-related projects, such as your overwhelming monthly report, for example, set aside specific times in your calendar to work on your novel. A half hour every day, or an hour every other day. List it as "Top Priority Project: NVL" in your calendar. And just like you have to show up at that meeting or work on that report so as to finish it by the deadline, make sure you adhere to your schedule and work on your true "Top Priority Project" at the designated times.

- Commit to writing a certain number of words each day while at the office, be it five hundred or a thousand or more. Hold firm that you cannot leave the office until you have fulfilled your commitment. You'll find a way to make the time—especially if you're like most worker-bots and like to get the hell out of the office right at quitting time.

- Just like smokers trying to quit throw a piece of gum in their mouths every time they feel the impulse to light up, every time you open up your browser to check out a gossip site or the blog you

WORKING FOR THE MAN RULE #119 • If someone spills a large cup of soup—a concoction with lots of garlic and onions—he'll do it right in front of your cube. It will sink into the carpet and stink up your space for days.

WORKING FOR THE MAN RULE #120 • See the movie *Ikiru* by Akira Kurosawa. This movie might just be enough to inspire you to break out of the rote nature of your job and do something that actually matters.

are currently addicted to, fire up your word processing program and pound out a paragraph or two of writing.

• Dread meetings at work? Of course you do. Instead of re-running the *Star Wars* movies in your mind just to stay awake, jot down notes or bits of dialogue for your novel. If you can pull off writing actual paragraphs in that kind of environment, with someone blathering on and on and on, the more power to you. TIP: Look up every once in a while and make eye contact with whoever it is that is talking. All your writing will look like you are simply taking copious meeting notes.

• If you really, really hate your job, and you find yourself complaining to anyone who will listen, as well as making several calls a day to your significant other bitching and moaning about your sorry lot in life (not attractive!), you need to make a conscious decision to focus not on broadcasting your complaints but on writing your novel. Every time you feel the impulse to complain about most likely the same old shit, that should be the trip wire that sends you back to your desk to write. If you can pull this off, you will feel much better about yourself and your job (and people in the office, as well as your significant other, might actually want to talk to you again).

- If you are really focused on doing well at your job, and do indeed do a bang-up, kick-ass job, simply take that same standard for excellence and efficiency and find a way (while you are on the clock) to make it happen for your personal project as well: Prioritize time to work on your novel, and when you are working on it, give the words you write the high-level attention to detail, originality, and top-notch quality you would give an important work-related project.

- Take advantage of the lunch hour. Either find a quiet café and write in your journal, or write while you eat at your desk. Finding a café is preferable—gets you away from your ringing phone, incoming emails, people popping by to talk with you, not to mention that big old stack of papers that needs to be dealt with.

WORKING FOR THE MAN RULE #121 • It's not about how hard you work. It's about how hard people *think* you are working.

- Incorporate events and characters from the workplace into your story. Annoying coworkers and your boss will certainly provide loads of ideas. Writing them into your story has the added benefit of helping you mentally deal with their shit in the real working world: You'll find that taking the time to reveal the absurdities of your workplace in the form of the written word has a soothing effect—it provides a way to take a step back and laugh at the ridiculousness of it all.

WORKING FOR THE MAN
RULE #122 • Never learn how to change the toner in the printer or copy machine. That way, when someone comes up to you and asks, "Do you know how to change the toner?" you can say, "Nope."

Plus, there's that whole revenge thing: In the pages of your novel you can expose—in a no-holds-barred fashion—the idiotic and petty behavior of your terrible boss and lame coworkers to the reading public at large (or at least to the people in your office that you like).

- When working on your novel, spread out paperwork all over your desk. It will look like you are really busy, and if people stop by to talk with you about something, you can just point to all the papers and say, "I can't talk right now—I'm in deep." They'll totally get it, and leave you alone to write.

- Form a writing group with like-minded coworkers. Reserve a conference room each week and hold your workshop sessions right there during the middle of the workday.

- End your day with an allotted amount of time to write—say the last fifteen minutes or so before quitting time. It will clear your headspace of the day-job baggage and put you in a writing frame of mind as you head out the door. It's also a great way to reignite your energy level and find your second wind after a long day at work. You can then use that second wind to carry you home and continue with your writing efforts until it's time to hit the sack and begin the workday, I mean novel writing, anew.

OTHER PROJECTS YOU SHOULD COMPLETE WHILE YOU'RE ON THE CLOCK

This could be an endless list. It's as long as the countless number of dreams that are floating around in people's heads—some hatching, some not quite latched on to, many that will never be, and some that will come true beyond the wildest of wild imaginations.

It's strange to think of it this way, but the workplace setting is completely built around the concept of producing whatever it is that that particular company produces. It's a machine that, despite whatever dysfunction you witness (and most likely contribute to in your own special way), leads to an output, whether it's a product or service. There are many resources and tools that make this machine run. You should spend a considerable amount of time thinking about the ways in which you can harness these elements— from the design skills of a coworker to the office copy machine—to help drive your own, personal projects. Some of these projects might be:

Write a screenplay. You know, the one you're always talking about at parties, but haven't really done any work on. Except the opening shot. You know exactly how to shoot that opening shot.

Start a collection of poetry. Your work-related downer moods

WORKING FOR THE MAN RULE #123 • Know who does know how to change the toner, and if he's a jerk, you can readily identify that person whenever someone is asking about getting the toner changed: "Jim knows. Go ask him."

and feelings of despair should lend themselves very well to your effort here.

Run a website. Create it around one of your main interests, and work to build an audience. If you truly love what you're writing about and put some real effort into it, you may be able to eventually parlay the website into other opportunities (such as a new job more closely tied to your interests), as well as generate some extra income.

Produce a play. From organizing the players and crew to printing the programs, use your office at work to put together the logistics of your show.

> **WORKING FOR THE MAN RULE #124** • Of course if you have no idea who actually knows how to change the toner, go ahead and specify the jerk on the floor, who may or may not know how to change the toner. Hopefully he'll be really busy and stressed out and in the middle of something really important.

Get the band together. Once you get past the "It's all about the music" phase, you can run the business of your band—booking shows, selling T-shirts, making MySpace friends—from your desk at work in between doing your non-music-related, gotta-pay-the-bills day-job duties.

Be an art star. You may not be able to paint a canvas or build a sculpture in your cubicle area, but you can sketch out your next project, design and send out postcards promoting your upcoming show, apply for artist grants, fellowships, or artist colony residencies, or update your website with the portfolio shots of your latest works.

Fill out graduate school applications. For those who haven't quite given up the whole novel-writing thing, but want to be more professionally tied to the written word (as if you'll be able to land a teaching gig if you get an MFA—yeah, right).

Fill out law school applications. For those who have given up the dreams of making it as a novelist. Hey, John Grisham has done quite nicely. Keep the dream alive!

Write your business plan. At the very least, you'll have lots of details on how *not* to run a company.

Run a side business. From selling things on eBay or Etsy .com to some kind of a consultancy, you have the benefit of the company you work for paying a lot of your expenses, like long distance phone calls and shipping.

THE PROCRASTINATION LIST

This is going to be either pure genius or extremely pathetic—and perhaps both at the same time. Chronicle all those things that you do all day long to avoid the work at hand—from checking IMDb.com to see what the actors from *The Greatest American Hero* are up to, to looking at your vacation photos from last year at your online photo account. Write it all down. Expose the true nature of a day's work. Unlock the mystery of "where all the time goes," and discover why (or rather how) that project didn't get done on time. The list serves two purposes: a reminder of what not to do, so that you stay focused and on task, as well as a menu of items to avoid work and help make the day go by faster. Most likely, it will come in handy for the latter.

WORKING FOR THE MAN
RULE #125 • Your flight out of [insert name of your least favorite city], where you were forced to go to placate an unreasonable client, will get delayed.

WORKING FOR THE MAN
RULE #126 • At the airport in which you are stranded, all the restaurants in the food court will be closed.

Some common activities that will be on most people's procrastination list:

- Online research on relieving your back pain
- Dusting your shelves
- Googling your exes
- Online search for the latest celebrity sex tape to hit the web
- Checking out the blog of your current cyber-crush
- Updating your Netflix account
- Getting up multiple times to look at the hottie who may or may not be a new hire
- Calls to your health insurance company to find out why you keep getting lab testing/doctor visit bills that should be covered by your plan
- Asking a coworker over and over if he thinks the layoffs are coming
- Online research for tips on how to prevent your chronic carpal tunnel syndrome pain
- Checking your webmail account
- Calling significant other just to "See what's going on"
- Recycling old reports that you never read in the first place
- Checking to see if you have any new MySpace "Friend Requests"
- Cleaning out your inbox
- Organizing files on your hard drive
- Making a fresh to-do list

SEX MESSAGING

You may not have physical access to your significant other, but that doesn't mean you have to go completely without during your time on the clock. You can text message your dirtiest fantasies via a mobile device. Unlike phone sex, in which people might be able to overhear your conversations, text messaging is something you can do in a private way even when you are in a very public space with no privacy, such as in your cubicle. Using an IM tool on your computer is always an option, but text messaging allows you to continue the sex messaging even when you are sitting around a conference table talking about Q2 strategies with the bigwigs.

You can always try to get the Triple XXX talk going with the ol' "What r u wearing?" opening line, but it's best to get your partner on board ahead of time and agree that on a particular day, you are going to get each other's freak on via text message. That's not very spontaneous, but at least you won't get a reply to your first message that is the equivalent of the "I have a headache" excuse, something like: "In mtgs all day, c u after work."

Though this sex messaging has a way of helping to rapidly eat up some of the minutes you have to be at work, it might also make the day feel like it is never going to end, so badly do you want to get home and see your partner in the flesh. But

WORKING FOR THE MAN

RULE #127 • You will be on that trip with the most obnoxious coworker, and he will not stop saying, "I can't believe our flight was delayed. I can't believe our flight was delayed. Can you believe this? I mean, can you? I can't believe our flight was delayed."

regardless, once you and your partner do finally get together, you'll both be ready and ripe to rip each other's clothes off and have some mind-blowing sex. Knowing that the extended foreplay was done while you were both on the clock will take it to an even higher orgasmic level.

OPTION: Put your phone camera feature to use and start sending each other visuals to go with your text messages. Sneak into the bathroom or close your office door for privacy, so you can give your shots just the right erotic charge, or, what the hell, a flat-out gratuitous shock. Regarding transmission of said photos: As the buttons are small and the clicking interface somewhat cumbersome, be doubly sure you are sending to your significant other, and not, for example, your boss, or even worse, everyone in your contacts list. And delete the evidence immediately! You don't want these pictures hanging around on your phone only to surface when, months from now, your mother borrows your phone and somehow stumbles into your photo archives, only to be flashed by your grainy but all too clear business.

> **WORKING FOR THE MAN**
> **RULE #128** • Once your finally do get on a plane, you coworker will promptly fall asleep and begin to snore—complete with frequent grunts and drooling—like a wild boar.

LUNCH HOUR+ (NOTE THE PLUS!)

Organize trips to restaurants farther and farther away from the office. Start getting more and more people to go—all in the name of office camaraderie, and maybe just a little of stretching the lunch hour and shortening the workday.

Just like Kramer in that episode of *Seinfeld* where he and the car salesman see how far they can go with their car's gas gauge on and then beyond the big "E"—see just how far out and for how long you can get all your coworkers to go.

HOW NOT TO START THE DAY OFF IN A BAD MOOD

The way you feel first thing in the morning has a huge impact on how the rest of your day will unfold. Wake up feeling good and ready to roll, there's a good chance you'll stay on the upswing and have a great day, but if you start out in a bad mood, it's likely that it will get worse as the day wears and tears its way to a bitter end. So you don't want to wake up on the wrong side of the bed, and more important, you don't want to be told by that annoying twit in your office that "Geez, you sure did wake up on the wrong side of the bed." The following is a guide on how to start the day out right.

Yes, you should wake up right when that alarm clock goes off, instead of hitting the snooze bar over and over again and reliving that sinking feeling that you have to get your ass up out of bed. The one exception is if you are staying in bed for some sex.

Once you do get out of bed, you should brush your teeth. For

WORKING FOR THE MAN RULE #129 • But before he actually doses off, he will have removed his shoes, and the smell of his sweaty, stinking feet—finally unleashed from his cheap leather shoes—will keep you awake and nauseated the entire flight.

the love of God, brush your teeth. And do it first thing, so that you don't walk around as if you are still asleep with that terrible taste and bad breath feeling in your mouth.*

You should say, "Good morning, sunshine!" to your significant other, and not "Is there no more fucking coffee? Are you fucking kidding me? Don't tell me you didn't pick up any coffee, because I will fucking lose it! Is there really no more coffee? I mean, that is so like you, so like you. I cannot BELIEVE there is no fucking coffee in this house . . ."

You should eat a nutritious breakfast—a banana, a yogurt, and maybe some toast.

If you really want to go all-out, make some pancakes or French toast—do the Sunday morning thing but on a workday. Leave the dishes for later.**

*If you are staying in bed for sex, should you ruin the spontaneity by getting up and first brushing your teeth? Does everyone do this in real life, and what we see in the movies—gorgeous couples waking up and doing the nasty with some serious face mashing, even though they both would clearly have that terrible morning death breath—just throws us off? Personal preference, I suppose. Spontaneity versus fresh breath. A toss-up that will go one way one day, another way the next.

**If you leave the dishes, it may cause a fight with your partner/roommates when you come home at the end of your day—but hey, if you start the day off in a good mood, you'll be able to handle this little end-of-day skirmish.

You should not turn on the television and watch those crap morning shows with those annoying morning-show "families" acting so giddy and silly and all "Hey, look at us, America, we're having fun, fun, fun!"

Go to the gym, or go for a run. If you can do this regularly and make it a daily ritual, you are going to feel and look like a million dollars. You will also be both admired and despised by those who know about your early morning workouts (temper the frequency with which you discuss/announce how awesome you feel due to your very disciplined a.m. exercise accomplishments). Note that when you first begin this routine, you will feel exhausted by about 1 p.m., and will want nothing more than to take a nap. You may actually find yourself waking up from an inadvertent nap—hopefully not because your boss is giving you a nudge, or doing one of those exaggerated clearing-of-the-throat maneuvers. But once you get over the hump of those difficult early efforts and it simply becomes a part of your daily routine, you are going to give yourself a very in-shape leg up on starting out the day right.

Shower without the rush. Let the water wash over your face and body and just let it keep on coming. Breathe in the steam and really let the hot water do its magic on your nerves. If possible, and to further expand the soothing, spalike quality of your experience, why not invite your partner in for some shower sex?

To *really* ensure that you start the day off right, you should play *your* song, your morning song, the one that shakes and rattles you in your core, the one that makes you feel like you should be running really fast and maybe winning some kind of race, the one that makes you dance, the one that makes you sing in the mirror, the one that makes you feel like if you were in a fight you'd bust out with some serious martial arts moves and kick some serious ass and not even get a finger laid on you, the one that makes you feel like you just want to get up and go and take on the day.

Some suggestions:

- **"Under Pressure" by David Bowie and Queen.** It's always something, right? There's always pressure to do this, to do that, you screwed this up, or didn't screw it up but everyone is blaming you anyway, and just how are you going to get it all done anyway? This song makes you feel like you can take that weight and more. Bring it on, man, bring it on.
- **"Born to Run" by Bruce Springsteen.** The way this song starts, a clunked up jam that stumbles its way into a raucous symphony of musical thunder, makes you want to dance around and pump your fists and scream "Baby we were born to run."
- **"Don't Stop 'Til You Get Enough" by Michael Jackson.** Man, this song is a party. You have no choice but to get up and groove. Even if you think you can't dance—if you are that person who avoids the dance floor at weddings—this song will have you sliding across the floor and swaying your way into the day feeling groovy.

- **"Vacation" by The Go-Go's.** Good-times beat with just the right amount of thump and sugary sweetness, and no, you aren't going on vacation, but this song will put you in a vacation frame of mind. And hey, the name of the band could not be more apt.

Of course everyone is different. You know your song, or songs. Queue it up, push play, and pump up the volume.*

You should leave on time, so that you don't have to stress about how you are going to be late the entire way to work. Unless, of course, you're still in that honeymoon phase of your relationship, and you and your partner decide to have sex not once but twice in the a.m.—one of those just-about-to-leave, ah-hell-with-it, let's-fuck-again-right-here-by-the-door, who-

---

*If you and your partner have very different tastes in music, then your pumping up the volume on *your* song is sure to trigger one of those heated "You better turn that SHIT off right FUCKING NOW!" arguments. And you may feel that that song *defines* who you are at the core, and there your partner is, dismissing it in such a loud and obnoxious way. Escalation potential is high here, with horrible things you did six or seven years ago getting brought up in high decibels. Your whole morning, not to mention your day, could get ruined. So be cool. Try to pick a song that the entire household will dig. Universally loved songs with strong pump up viability: "Video Killed the Radio Star" by Buggles, "Come On Eileen" by Dexys Midnight Runners, "99 Luftballons" by Nena, "Just Can't Get Enough" by Depeche Mode.**

**If your partner does not like one of the above listed universally loved songs—which transcend the *I'm too cool to like what everyone else likes* mentality—then it's time to seriously reconsider your entire relationship. It would be like being seriously involved with someone who does not like the movie *Footloose*. Time to move on. Then you can listen to whatever music you want to.

cares-if-the-shades-are-open-and-anyone-looking-in-the-
windows-can-see-us-here-screwing-like-wild-dogs-on-the-
hardwood-floor fucks.

Bring in donuts for your coworkers. You might not like all
of them, but there's something about a gesture like this that
just makes everyone smile, and for a brief moment, you can
feel magnanimous and good about yourself for being so gen-
erous, instead of the selfish, discombobulated nugget of complaints and misery that you are most of the time.*

After you are done being magnanimous, or 90 percent
magnanimous (depending on what you did with that last
donut), turn on your computer, but instead of looking at all
your emails and checking voice mail messages, get right to
work on something you actually like doing. It may be work
work, or it might be a few paragraphs on your novel—just
make sure the first thing you do once you settle into your
chair is something you actually like doing.

Now you're ready to make your way through the day.
Starting it off in a good mood is the surest way to make it so
that you'll actually have a nice day or, at the very least, help
you take the crap and just roll it off your back. This is work,
after all: You're gonna get kicked, just make sure they aren't
kicking you when you're down.

---

*Of course, if there's that one guy who you simply cannot stand and it's actu-
ally going to get under your skin that he's going to get something nice from
you, make sure this total and complete asshole just misses getting the very
last donut. "Oh, I'm sorry, Jim . . . I thought I had bought enough . . . The last
maple bar just got taken . . ."

HOW TO HANDLE THE VARIOUS MOODS AT WORK

There are so many moods at work that you experience on a daily basis. Feeling exhausted, pissed off at being outmaneuvered or shut out, overwhelmed, bored out of your mind, wishing it was Friday, dreading a long meeting, wondering if the day is ever going to fucking end. We're all different in how we handle the various moods; we all have our own quick fix or cure.

But sometimes you end up paralyzed, sitting at your desk, on the verge of either falling asleep, shedding tears, or just grabbing up that old giant monitor—"Why does everyone have a flat screen but me?" you scream to yourself—and hurling it against the wall.

It's helpful to keep a little list of your fixes—a reminder to yourself to get out of your chair and do that simple thing that can turn your mood in a more upward direction.

First, let's just list the various moods, to fully illustrate the emotional roller coaster you can experience during just one simple day at work:

- You're exhausted first thing in the morning, and the tired ache is down to the bone.
- You have too many emails / the emails won't stop.
- Annoying coworkers might not even say anything to you, but just the sight of them pushes your buttons.
- You have long meeting dread.
- You are possessed by the knowledge that you are going to have to stay late.

- You feel anxiety because you are most certainly not going to be getting an assignment done in time.
- Your boss tells you that you're doing a horrible job, and you go back to your desk and feel sort of like someone died.
- Your boss tells you that you're doing a great job, then proceeds to give you a whole list of things you need to get done—not a promotion, not a raise, just more of the same crap work!
- You keep repeating, "I just need a vacation." Especially scary if you just got back from one.
- Caffeine headache—you've either drunk too much or not enough.
- Starving—at first you think you might be getting sick, but then you realize you're feeling that way because you haven't had time to go grab lunch.
- Bleary-eyed and wiped out because you've been staring at spreadsheets for hours, and you aren't even close to being done.
- You have an after-lunch food coma.
- You surf the web, go get water, head to the bathroom, run down and get another cup of coffee, then go back to surfing the web—you just can't seem to get started.
- The day won't end. It feels like it was 4:30 p.m. several hours ago, but it's only 1:30.

Now the quick fixes. And the point is, these really are quick fixes—things you can do on a moment's notice. Again, everyone is different. Read these over and then come up with your own list.

- **Take a trip to the vending machine.** Nothing like a little sugar pick-me-up to make you feel a little better. Buy something for a coworker and drop it off on your way back to your desk. Your coworker is probably having her own version of a bad day, and your little surprise will probably bring a smile to her face. Improving her mood will improve your mood even more.
- **Coffee break.** It's not just about the caffeine jolt— it's nice to get away from your desk with the simple task of getting a hot cup of joe. Don't rush back into the office. Take a moment to sip it down and let the warmth of the coffee take its effect—a nice combination of soothing and energizing.
- **Walk around the building.** Nothing like a bit of fresh air to calm your nerves and help put things in perspective—it's just work, after all. You really shouldn't be getting so worked up.
- **Take a long lunch.** Sometimes you just have to treat yourself to a nice, long, expensive lunch, even if you can't really afford the time or the tab. You know when you deserve a reward like this, and it's unlikely anyone else is going to offer to take you out, so make an executive decision to take yourself out to lunch.
- **Surf *Colbert Report* clips on YouTube.com.** Guaranteed to make you laugh. Sometimes all it takes to

let go of your anger and frustration is to have a good
laugh.

- **Go see a matinee movie.** If you can swing it without
  being noticed or without getting in trouble, head out
  of the office and catch a flick.

- **Send sexy IMs to your partner.** (See Sex Messaging
  on page 169.)

- **Plan a vacation.** Spending a little time planning
  your next vacation can give you something to look
  forward to—a reminder that that island does exist,
  and that you will be lying on its beaches, sipping ice
  cold beer after ice cold beer in the not-so-distant
  future.

- **Job hunt.** (See The On-The-Clock Job Hunt on page
  213.)

- **Arrange a drink (or drinks) after work.** With your
  coworkers, your friends, your significant other, or all
  of the above.

GENERAL TIPS AND TRICKS FOR EVERYDAY USE

The one upside to the monotony of your daily work experience is that you can be fully prepared for what's coming. And
being prepared can take some weight off of that monotony,
which has a way creating a dreadful, sinking feeling. Here are
some simple, straightforward things you can do or be aware
of to ease the pressure, lighten your load, and make your
workaday dealings run a little smoother:

- Do not bring a briefcase, backpack, or heavy bag to
  the office when arriving late, so that if you do bump

into your boss in the elevator, you can just say, "What a morning, I'm already on my second cup of coffee."

- Leave on time (it's only right, since you are required to be there at a certain time). Learn to become immune to the cold stare—a combination of anger, disgust, and disbelief—from your boss as you pack up your bag, turn off your computer, and walk out the door.

- If you do happen to stay late at the office, make sure to send out a heavily CC'd email (making sure to include your boss) right before you leave, so that your sacrifice is documented by the time stamp on the email.

- Find a picture of yourself where you look really happy, perhaps surrounded by friends and family. Put that picture up on your bulletin board or framed on your desk.

- On the next outing or event with your coworkers and boss, take lots of group pictures. Hopefully you'll nail one where your boss looks like an idiot. Make duplicates of the photo and hand them out to everyone, and be sure to post the picture up on your own bulletin board.

- Keep an emergency granola bar in your desk. That way, you avoid the guilt of eating a candy bar from the office vending machine, and it gives you quick access to food when you're starving and either stuck at your desk on deadline or rushed into a last-minute two-hour-long meeting.

- Check out Lifehacker.com, 43folders.com, Lifehack .org, SolutionWatch.com, and SlackerManager.com for tips, tricks, and hacks on how to make your working life easier.

- Always keep two aspirin at the ready. If there's one thing that's guaranteed about work, it's a pounding headache at the worst possible time. Don't make that headache worse by having to go on a frustrating hunt for someone who will both be at his desk *and* have some aspirin to spare.

- The best strategy you can have for a strategy session meeting is to come up with a solid excuse to get out of it.

- Never answer your phone after 4:30 p.m. That's prime time for last-minute, urgent issues that involve someone else's emergency. These calls totally throw off the end of your day and keep you at the office well past the time you were planning to leave. Just listen to the possibly panicky voice mail and plan your response (or your non-response) carefully. Don't let yourself get put on the spot or duped into staying late.

THINGS YOU CAN DO AT WORK TO SAVE MONEY

You work your job so you can make money. But you should also see your job as a way to implement cost-savings into your life. That's just a businesslike way of saying that your office offers up all kinds of things that you can take advantage of, free and clear, so that you don't have to tap the hard-earned bucks in your wallet. The more opportunities you seize in this area, the more disposable income you'll have, meaning you'll have a greater amount of money to spend on beer and vacations and fancy clothes and whatever else you want.

Make long distance phone calls. This is part of the plan on your cell phone, but until they get cell phone service up to par, or even close to par, it's nice to use a landline every once in a while—no "Can you hear me now?" or "Are you still there?" comments interspersed throughout the call. Do it at the office so you don't have to pay the long distance charges. Especially if it's an international call.

Supply your home office with office supplies. It's like Christmastime after a really good year in terms of office supplies around the office: rubber bands, pens (the good kind, not those cheap, smear-prone pens), paper, paper clips, tape, scissors, staples, binders, and more. Only a chump buys this stuff on his own dime.

Get paper towels. You shouldn't be buying paper towels, on account of the environment—but if your company insists on having a good supply, why not put them to use at the homestead? You can cut your guilt by half, because technically, you didn't actually purchase the paper towels.

Get toilet paper. Of course they do it because it's the cheapest stuff around, but it seems, or rather feels, more like a sinister plot: stocking the most abrasive toilet paper in every single bathroom stall in corporate America. But when you aren't able to make ends meet, desperate measures are necessary, and that means taking home rolls of toilet paper from the office stock. The good news is this stuff doubles as sandpaper—so you're covered if you happen to have any wood projects in the works.

Secure your candy fixes. Yes, there's that vending machine stocked with all kinds of goodies, but why pay for it when scattered throughout the office, there are those kindly coworkers who put out jars of candy and other types of treats. Make a strong mental note of who these folks are and where they sit, so you can strategically hit them up to satisfy your sugar cravings. Also, the Publicity Department is usually good about stocking their pantry with all manner of snacks— pretzels, suckers, microwavable popcorn, licorice. Raid it when you get the serious munchies.

Mail things. Think of the company mail room as a post office—except you don't stand in line, nor do you pay for stamps or shipping fees. Excellent for sending not only letters and bills, but party or wedding invites, not to mention any side project mailings (review copies, shipping to customers, press releases). Note that utilizing the company's shipping options will help you really save some dollars around the holidays, as well as if you have to overnight something or send a package internationally. Tape up your personal mailings very securely, and make sure you put the right addresses on your labels—you don't want the stuff to get sent back and opened up by someone other than you.

Photocopy things. If you're in your zine-making phase, then free access to the company photocopier is absolutely key—a little slice of heaven in an otherwise corporate world of drear. The hum of the machine—assuming it's not jamming every two minutes—is an electric pleasure, and you can't help but smile as your hard work is spit out free page after free page. If you're not a zinester, making free copies is always a nice option—because it's tax time, or maybe you need to make copies for a class you are taking, a "For Sale" sign you are posting all over town, a flyer for a show you are promoting, or because you just have a bunch of personal documents to copy.

Use company cars. While they're mostly reserved for the sales force, if you have the option of getting a company car, take it, use it, and abuse it just within having to pay for anything out of your own pocket. It's nice to drive a car around that is essentially like a rental—you don't have to worry about putting too much mileage on it, or the little noises the engine has started to make. The decreased value or cost of repairs is all on the company.

Get discounts. Often companies will arrange it so their employees get discounts on membership at local gyms—if that's the case, take advantage of it. And if that's not the case, then ask your Human Resources department to make some inquiries and negotiate some deals. Usually HR is there to serve management. This is a positive way to encourage the so-called Human Resources department to serve the actual human resources of the company.

Speaking of HR, you most likely ignore the "Company All" emails you get from that department, things along the lines of "Come Learn About Email Etiquette!" so you probably miss announcements about corporate discounts available to you for museums, movies, theater, and more. These discounts are worth knowing about and taking advantage of, so be sure to check in every once in a while with HR (hopefully through the company's intraweb) to see what money-saving opportunities are available to you for the various entertainment options in your locale.

Get leftovers. Start mapping out where the sandwiches, chips, and sodas leftover from the bigwig meetings get placed. Usually that stuff is placed in the pantry areas on the floors where the biggest, nicest conference rooms are located. Yes, it's scrounging, but it makes no sense to pay $5 to $10 for a bad sandwich at the same old places for lunch every day when you can get decent food for free. As mentioned in the People to Kiss Up To section on page 29, getting the when and whereabouts of these free food deposits is much more efficient if you make nice with the person responsible for arranging the catered lunches—usually the executive assistants.

Extend corporate trips into vacations. If you have to travel for work, make sure to coordinate it so that you can spend some non-work-related days enjoying the places that you have to go to—either staying through the weekend or using a vacation day or two. This way, your company pays for the airfare, and possibly some of the hotel bill. And while you're on these business trips, get smart about how you spend your per diems—try to spend as little of the money as possible while you're on the clock, so that you can either pocket the cash or use it during the extended portion of the trip when you're just enjoying yourself and not thinking about work in the slightest.

Expense your lunches. You have to be strategic about it, and you have to always be able to back it up with a receipt *and* a credible story, but if you've got an expense account, figure out how to expense your lunches as often as possible, and at the finest restaurants to boot. List out the restaurants you want to hit, the friends you want to take, and add a third column to strategically justify each lunch that you plan to take. If you're stupid about this, it will all fall apart, but if you're smart about it, and stay away from obvious abuse, you—and your friends—will be eating like kings on the man's dollar. There's no such thing as a free lunch . . . in life—that still holds, but there is such thing as a free lunch for you . . . when your expense account is involved.

THINGS YOU CAN DO TO MAKE THE DAY GO BY FASTER

You've got to show up, and you've got to put in your time. No way around it. The key is to make the time you put in move along as quickly as possible. Here are some tips and tricks to get you through your day with maximum expediency:

Arrive late. But not in a huffing, puffing, sweating defeatist way. Stop off and grab some breakfast somewhere. Maybe pick up a coffee and read the paper at your favorite cafe.

Run some personal errands. Not dental floss, shaving cream, and a new toothbrush—something fun—new clothes, new shoes, a gift for your partner.

Organize those online photo albums you've been meaning to arrange. Write good captions. Make the slideshow a real show.

Get a haircut. Afterward, treat yourself to a manicure.

Research and download music to make the perfect mix tape. Give each song a thorough listen to get the compilation just right.

Go get coffee. Like four or five times over the course of the afternoon.

Clean out your inbox. And then clean out your personal webmail account's inbox.

Post a "Do Not Disturb" sign on your door. It should indicate you are doing something very important—"Speaking on live web event." Then, take a nap.

Leave early. Not in a stressful way, and not in a way that has you sneaking down the hall hoping you don't bump into your boss in the elevator. Have somewhere fun to go and a good excuse to get you out the door well before quitting time.

MEMO

events at work that can immediately ruin your day

- An announcement is made that your office building will not have water for three days. Everyone figures that they will be given three days off. That's the rumor floating around the office. People even start making plans, putting together little mini-vacations. But then a memo is passed out explaining that you will all have temporary access to the bathroom facilities in the building across the street.

- Your boss shows up on the day she usually works from home.

- Your coworker comes out of the boss's office crying, and you are absolutely thrilled, thinking that she has finally been reprimanded for her horrible work habits. But then you are called into the boss's office and told that you need to make sure you say hello to people when they arrive at work, and that you need to be "nicer" around the office. When you ask why you are being told to say hello to coworkers, you are told that "some people" have complained that you are making them uncomfortable by ignoring them.

- Your boss shows up. It isn't his day off, but you were just really hoping he wouldn't come in today.

- You are working on a report that you have been slaving on for days. Your boss keeps adding new data, which is forcing you to rework the entire report over and over again. Somehow, just as you are nearing completion, you lose the file—you're not sure if you deleted it or overwrote it or if something is wrong with your computer. Not even an emergency assist from Tech Support can locate the file. All you know is that it's gone and you will now have to do the whole thing over.

- For two solid hours you are convinced that it is Friday, even dating several letters with Friday's date. Then, like a loud scream thrust unexpectedly in your face, you realize it's only Thursday. Your heart sinks and your stomach aches like you are hungry and homesick at the same time.

- Instead of taking the usual three hours to get the computers back up and running after a network crash, it only took the tech guys five minutes to get the system back online. Back to work!

- On a Friday morning your boss walks in with a huge grin on her face and tells everyone she's got some great news. The firm has just landed a major new account! Everyone claps, it's smiles all around. Then she explains that there's a big meeting on Monday, and that everyone needs to come into the office and burn the midnight oil through the weekend in order to get a pull-out-all-the-stops presentation ready for the client.

- After everyone in the office is given a free muffin and an orange juice for breakfast—delivered right to each person's desk—you start to make fun of management's efforts to reward everyone for their hard work. "Let them have their little muffins and tiny juice cartons," you say in a mock-haughty voice to your coworkers. Then, as you stand up to get a little more into the act, you spill your juice all over your pants, and as you jump away in an attempt to avoid getting completely drenched, you knock your muffin onto the floor. You are hungry and thirsty, but too embarrassed to ask for another muffin and orange juice.

- Just sitting at your desk, you have one of those bone-chilling revelations that strike for no reason in particular, that the work you do is totally meaningless and you will be showing up in an office just like the one you are in right then, sitting at the same kind of desk, doing the same old meaningless work, for a long, long time.

No matter how prepared you are, no matter how happy you think you'll be once you are truly free of the place, it's always unsettling—even humiliating—getting the boot.

There's nothing more telling about the coldhearted nature of the world of work than the way in which a company rids itself of its 113th priority. That's right—employees rank pretty low on the scale of importance, well below the CEO, management, stockholders, advertisers, servers, and office supplies (not necessarily staples or tape, but definitely well below an item such as color toner).

Perhaps it's incompetence, that you didn't fit in, that you totally deserved the ax. Could be that you didn't get along with your boss. Possibly the company is "reorganizing." Maybe you're too old and get too high of a salary. (*Isn't that illegal?* you are thinking. Please. They'll find a way to get rid of you.) Whatever it is, there is no loyalty in the workplace anymore, and you'd be a fool to think otherwise. But hey, truly understanding the tenuous hold you

**WORKING FOR THE MAN
RULE #131** • Taping a penny
to a piece of paper, writing
"Thanks for the bonus this
year!" on it, and then hanging
it up on the outside of your
cubicle is not the best way to
express your opinion about the
bonus you didn't get this year.

have on your job is not a bad
thing—indeed, it's one of the
keys to handling the insecurity
you might feel due to your lack
of job security. Following are
some additional ways to manage
those unexpected, unceremoni-
ous exits and get you safely
across burned bridges to greener
pastures.

to-do list

YOUR OFFICE GO-KIT

In this day of color-coded terrorist alerts, we're supposed to
have a go-kit at the ready in our homes, in case we need to
leave at a moment's notice due to some kind of terrorist at-
tack. This go-kit concept is something similar to the bag
pregnant women who are approaching their due date have
near the front door. Well, in this day of massive layoffs and
corporate fraud (Is it really any different than any other
time? No, it's not.), as well as the possibility that you'll simply be summarily fired without notice, it's important to think
ahead and have your office go-kit at the ready. You may not
actually be able to pack it in advance, but you should definitely put together a readily available checklist, and that's
where the One Box Strategy comes in. To follow this strategy,
all you need to do is be able to throw all of your personal be-
longings, from the framed picture of your pets to your yoga

mat, into just one box, because you never know when you
might get fired and have just five minutes—all under the
watchful eye of an HR representative—to clear out your desk
and leave the building. Preparedness is everything. Write out
your checklist now.

NOTE: You most likely won't be allowed to delete files off
of your hard drive or copy impor-
tant files or your contacts. Be sure
to regularly (every month at least)
make updated copies of any information that you'd like to have access to even after you've left the
job, by storing the information on a
rewritable CD or portable storage
device (some of which are smaller
than a pen and can fit in your shirt
pocket).

> **WORKING FOR THE MAN**
> **RULE #132** • Don't get mad
> when your idiotic coworkers
> somehow start getting
> assistants. View these new hires
> as a protective layer of fat for
> that first round of layoffs that is
> surely right around the corner.

LIST ALL THE WAYS YOU'VE BEEN FIRED
OR LAID OFF

You most likely have quite a few firing/laid-off stories of your
own, but consider collecting the stories of your colleagues
and coworkers. You'll have a full-view picture of not only the
way companies and corporations, not to mention bad managers, inept HR representatives, and terrible bosses, discard,
cut, and fire their employees, but also the churning, chewing
underbelly of the workplace itself. Understanding the system
is the key to beating the system. Well, probably not. But
at least you'll be made more aware of the various ways your

WORKING FOR THE MAN
RULE #133 • "Mavericks" at
work are celebrated in books
and magazines, but in the
actual day-to-day workplace,
"Mavericks" get fired.

current and future companies
might sever their ties with you, allowing you to be more prepared
for a firing you aren't necessarily
supposed to see coming.

Here's a list of common ways
that people get the boot (possibly
also serving as a way to jog your memory of your own, personal experiences):

- You are called and just told, plain and simple, not to
  come in again, that your things will be sent to you
  (and of course, no box ever arrives).
- You get an email telling you that "Your position has
  been eliminated," and that a Human Resources representative will be in contact with you via phone or
  email with further details regarding the end of your
  employment with the company.
- Your boss, with that smirk you've always wanted to
  really, truly knock off his face, calls you into his office and says, flatly, "You're fired." He doesn't say
  anything more, just keeps that smirk on his face and
  has that look in his eyes like he's just been dying to
  tell you that.
- You are called up to Human Resources out of the
  blue and told that "The company is making a decision to end your employment." Then, you are walked
  back to your desk and given a few minutes to collect
  your things, all under the watchful eye of a security

guard or someone from HR, before being escorted out of the building.

- You go to log onto your computer, only to find out that your password no longer works. When you call Customer Support, you're told in an odd, mysterious way that someone from HR will be contacting you shortly. When you persist in your questioning, the call gets very uncomfortable, and the poor guy on the other end of the line, who knows damn well that you've been locked out of your computer because you're about to get the boot, just loses his patience and says, "Look, dude, HR is going to be calling you any minute . . . someone should have already called you . . . That's all I can say!"

- You are invited to an "all-hands" meeting, told by the president of the company that layoffs are coming, and then told that over the next "several months" management will be eliminating positions from every department. So for the next several months, the thing people focus on most is not their work, but who is and is not going to get laid off.

- You are invited to what seems like an "all-hands" meeting, but you soon realize that while it's a large group of people, not everyone has been invited. You are then told that either (1) your job is

> **WORKING FOR THE MAN**
> **RULE #134** • "Yes men" at work don't get celebrated in books and magazines, but in the actual day-to-day workplace, yes men get promoted.

safe and everyone who was not invited to the meeting will be laid off, or (2) everyone in the room is being laid off, and please go back to your desk and await a call from Human Resources.

- You are invited to an "all-hands" meeting and told by the president that in order to "stay competitive," the company is downsizing. She explains that you all should go back to your desks and that those whose positions are being eliminated will be receiving a call from Human Resources. Naturally, every time your phone rings, you panic, and of course your phone is ringing off the hook: It's either a friend wondering if you've gotten a call from HR, or a friend just trying to freak you out by making your phone ring.

- You show up to work and find that the doors are not only locked, but chain-linked together.

BREAKING THE NEWS

If you do get laid off, don't be the guy who walks around like it's the end of the world. That's just pathetic. It is, quite simply, not the end of the world. Not even close. Still, there is that issue of having to deliver the news of your layoff to pretty much everyone you know: partners, friends, family, and colleagues, including those people who might be just a little too happy about your predicament. That does suck. You have to worry about overly dramatic concern, not-so-helpful job ideas, shit-eating-grin condolences, and possible tirades about what a loser you are. In fact, it's these very conversations that give rise to the possibility of you becoming that end-of-the-world guy.

With that in mind, here are some ice breakers that will help you maintain control and perhaps spin the situation in a more positive direction as you spread the news about getting laid off:

To your wife: "Well it looks like I won't be buying those new golf clubs—the ones you said I didn't need or deserve—after all."

To your husband: "No, this certainly isn't a blessing in disguise. I'm still not ready to have a baby," or "And no, this does not mean we won't be able to afford the trip to visit my parents."

To your mother: "Tell Dad not to try to get me to call Uncle Harry for a job."

To your father: "Dad! I don't care if there's still a position open at Uncle Harry's insurance agency!"

To that coworker you've had the hots for but never made a move: "You know, now that we aren't going to be working together anymore, I should get your home number . . . ," or "We should just leave right now and go get smashed-up drunk."

To the Human Resources hatchet man: "I'm really glad you gave that two-hour meeting on our stock options last month . . ."

To your boss: "Well, since I've been fired, I might as well tell you how I really feel: You are a total fucking moron!"

To your girlfriend: "Yeah, it sucks, but what I really want to know right now is what kind of underwear are you wearing?"

To your boyfriend: "I'm not wearing any underwear right now," or "Just so you know, my ex-boyfriend asked me what kind of underwear I was wearing after I got laid off the last time, and I didn't think it was sexy."

To the still-employed coworker who is feigning concern and acting like someone just died: "We're heading to the bar on the corner, and the drinks are on you, Mr. Paycheck."

To the annoying salesman who is acting like he cares: "Don't you have some calls to make?"

To the bartender at the corner bar: "We all look depressed because we just lost our jobs. What kind of break can we get on our drinks?"

To your friend at the *Wall Street Journal*: "This is off the record, but . . ."

THE NOT-TO-DO LIST

It's never fun to be told what you cannot and should not do, and the workplace environment is top flight at delivering these kinds of messages, loudly and clearly and in a don't-let-the-door-hit-you-on-the-way-out way. Here's a not-to-do list that is not about discipline or the whims of a passive-aggressive, insecure higher-up, but serves more as a beneficial checklist for yourself as you walk the rigid halls and arbitrary walls of the workplace, things that you "should not" do in order to hedge against all the standard operating forces working against you and your place in the office. You don't, after all, want to make it *easy* for your company to get rid of you, and adhering to the following will at least provide some semblance of a firmer leg to stand on when the ax starts swinging in your general direction.

- Do not get caught.
- Do not panic if you get caught.
- Do not admit anything.

- Do not discuss via email questionable, possibly un-ethical work issues or practices that you may or may not be involved in.
- Do not send any personal email through your work account. Use a webmail account.
- Do not IM on your work computer. All your instant messaging, meaning all your complaints about your boss and coworkers, your juvenile antics, and your inappropriate sexual commentaries, are preserved by your company, and will be used against you should the need for leverage ever arise.
- Do not say "nice thong" to a coworker, even if you think she's your good friend.
- Do not say "Hooker Red" when a coworker asks what you think of her nail polish color.
- Do not reply immediately to an email or voice mail message that upsets you.
- Do not tell coworkers about your personal blog or MySpace page, especially if you write honestly and openly about all the absurd things that occur at your workplace.
- Do not complain about your boss or a department or a coworker to someone whose loyalties are not known to you (and understand, of course, that loyalties are shifting all the time).
- Do not ever challenge someone's accusation of not finishing a project on time or correctly without confirming what you promised in a sent email.
- Do not have your pornography or sex toys shipped to your office—the "discreet" packaging is a dead

giveaway to the guys in the mailroom, who just love to create an "accidental" shipping rip that's just enough to let everyone know exactly what you've ordered.

- Do not surf porn sites or try to download the latest celebrity sex tape on your work computer.
- Do not think that you are irreplaceable.
- Do not think it's going to be one of your greatest moments of glory to scream "Well then I quit!" in front of the whole office.
- Do not ever tell your boss what you *really* think about one of his ideas. It's always "interesting" or "innovative" or "really, really great."
- Do not believe it's about hard work. It's about how you spin the work that you've done.
- Do not write and publish a book like the one you are currently reading.
- Do not assume anyone is ever going to give you credit for the work you've done.
- Do not try to explain why something went wrong. Talk about what went right.

getting fired: the tried-and-true Cluetrain manifesto

The signs don't really start out subtly. Indeed, it's pretty apparent when the company you work for is in free fall and heading toward the point of no return. Nonetheless, people still act a little surprised when they're handed a pink slip and a cardboard box. And however the current economy is being labeled in the media, whether the buzz is about a boom or bust, companies are closing up shop all the time. So here's a list of signs that indicate your company is about to tank. Consider this the tried-and-true Cluetrain Manifesto:

- A staff meeting is called in which the "exciting new direction" of the company is announced. The phrase "exciting opportunity for each and every one of us" is used at least thirty-seven times in the course of the thirty-minute meeting.

- A staff meeting is called within a week of the first one, in which the "exciting new direction" of the company is revised. It is described as "an even more exciting new direction." Use of the phrase "exciting opportunity for each and every one of us," however, is used only once, and it seems more like a slip of the tongue.

- First, the company was touted as a B-to-C (business-to-consumer) play. Then, of course, it transitioned itself into a B-to-B (business-to-business) enterprise. Employees begin to confide in each other that it's really a BS-to-BS—Bullshit to Bullshit.
- You overhear the people in the PR Department overanxiously stressing on every phone call: "We're not an Internet company. We're a technology company."
- Items you send to the laser printer keep getting printed out on résumé paper.
- Several senior managers resign. All use the excuse of having to take care of a sick parent.
- Someone actually says out loud that she found the book *Who Moved My Cheese?* helpful. Even stranger, no one ridicules this person and tries to make her feel stupid.
- People keep dashing out of the office every time their cell phones ring.
- A story about the ins and outs of unemployment insurance gets passed around the office.
- The techies start showing up in ties.
- Inboxes that used to be filled with memos and meeting arrangements are now full of forwarded jokes, "check out this website" notes, and job leads.
- It seems like every day a different coworker, out of the blue and without prompting, makes the following comment: "I feel like I'm rearranging the deck furniture on the *Titanic*."

- Water cooler banter is of the New Economy war story variety: ". . . I had this friend, and he just hung on until the very end. I mean the very end. He was one of the last ones in the office. He knew the office was going to be closed, but for like two months, he didn't do a thing. He just waited until he got the official word, which came on the same day the computers were being boxed up and shipped to the main office in California."
- Talk of getting drinks after work starts at 9:45 a.m., instead of 4:45 p.m.
- Your tight-ass manager who used to ride you about staying focused invites you to take a long lunch with him to catch a one o'clock movie.
- The office manager receives a request via email from the head office for a "computer equipment inventory."
- The mention of the words "stock options" brings an eruption of laughter from every corner of the office.

CHAPTER FOURTEEN

Getting a
New Job

When you get fired, of course you have to look for a new job. You've got no choice. But when you are employed—the best position to be in when seeking out a better job—most people avoid making the effort. It's funny how trapped we feel, so restrained in our misery that instead of doing the obvious—looking for a new job—we just sit there day after day and complain constantly, not only while we're on the clock, but at home as well. And the significant other just loves hearing all about it. She or he looks forward to coming home after her or his hard day at work and hearing the same old story about the same old people doing the same old things to make your sorry little life a living hell.

All of this could be totally avoided by taking the energy expended on being so negative and plowing it into a concerted effort to find a better gig. A job hunt does not have to be a bad thing, especially if you do it while you're on the clock—essentially meaning that you are getting paid by your current company, the one you don't like—Bonus!—to find employment with a new company.

Plus, finding a new job means you get to experience the glory of your two weeks' notice—the best two weeks you'll have at any job you ever hold.

to-do list

CAREER COUNSELING YOURSELF

Most people detest job hunting. They avoid it and keep putting it off week after week, sometimes year after year, no matter how miserable their current job is making them feel. While having to send out résumés and write tailor-made cover letters is a big part of this, as is that sense of impending rejection, the main reason for such deep-rooted negativity toward the job hunt is that people are insecure about the fact that they either (1) have no idea what it is that they want to do professionally, or (2) know what they want to do, but the road to get there seems filled with big obstacles and is outrageously, impossibly long.

> **WORKING FOR THE MAN**
> **RULE #135** • Books by "career coaches" pretty much all say the same thing. Even the titles of the books are essentially the same. If you've read one, you've read them all.

There are no easy answers, no quick solutions. You just have to take a long, hard look at your current situation and then formulate a plan, one that is not set in stone, but a plan nonetheless. And then take it step by step. Keep in mind, this isn't some big report you have to produce for your boss or some major initiative you have to pull off for your company. This is all about you, analyzing your current situation and mapping out what you'd really like to do long-term. Make it an engaging personal project, and break it down into manageable exercises that you can do on company time. In other words, get paid for some much-needed personal improvement. Following are some project ideas to kick-off your effort.

> **WORKING FOR THE MAN**
> **RULE #136** • Given that career coaches seem to be poaching the material of the career coaches before them, it can be inferred that taking their stale, uninspired advice will lead to unoriginal, mediocre, unremarkable careers of irrelevance.

- First, write down your thoughts about your job—what you like about it, what you hate about it, where you think it's going, and how it relates to what you truly want to accomplish with your life. Then, watch the movie *Ikiru* by Akira Kurosawa. Or, read the book *Post Office* by Charles Bukowski. Right after the movie, or after you finish reading the book, write down your thoughts about your job—what you like about it, what you hate about it, where you think it's going, and how it relates to what you truly want to accomplish with your life.

- Right when you arrive at work, immediately after flipping on your computer, but before you start checking your email (or the online version of the newspaper you read), write down what you have to get done that day. Detail all the calls you have to make and the numbers you have to crunch and the emails you have to write and reply to, as well as any reports you have to turn in or any other deadlines you have to meet. After you are done writing up this list, write down how you feel about your job.

- Take a picture of yourself first thing when you wake up Monday morning. Take another picture just before you leave for work, and another just after you sit down at your desk. Take pictures of yourself throughout the day at specific times. Be sure to take one just before you leave work for the day. Repeat the picture-taking for each day of the week—Monday through Friday. Upload the pictures into an online photo album and view sequentially as a slideshow, or order them in print form, organize in sequence, and then flip through the pictures. What do you see?

- Open up the résumé you have saved on your computer at work (you know you have it stored in a discreetly named file, somewhere on your hard drive). While you're on the clock, add in a new job at the end of your résumé. This is the job you want but do not have. What is the title? What are your responsibilities? What have you accomplished? After you've written out how your ideal job will look on your résumé, take some additional company time and realistically assess what it will take to land that job.

WORKING FOR THE MAN RULE #137 • Getting advice from a career coach is like finding life-changing direction from videos and booklets you bought after watching an infomercial at 3 a.m.

Write out the steps. Before you go home that day, take step 1. If you've still got any time left, write your letter of resignation. Date the letter. You just set your deadline.

- List and describe all the jobs you've ever mentioned when someone has asked, "What do you want to be when you grow up?" Remember that even after you've "grown up," people have still asked you that question. At the end of the list, write down your current job. How does it fit in?

- What's the one thing you always say either out loud or just under your breath as you walk into the office, storm out of your cube, or go from meeting to meeting:

WORKING FOR THE MAN RULE #138 • Most career coaches are writers who operate out of their homes. They most likely left their office jobs/"careers" because, just like you, they hated their boss, didn't get the promotion they deserved, weren't making enough money, and were lousy at dealing with the usual office politics. The difference is that you're still a sucker, and they've figured out how to get on the other side of that scenario.

"I need a new fuck'n job."
"I hate this job."
"I can't take it anymore."
"I really hate this place."
"I really hate working with these fucking morons."

Did your coworkers give you a T-shirt emblazoned

with your well-known bitch-and-moan statement? What's behind the vitriol? Write down the one thing you always say, and then list out all the reasons why you say it. Once the list is down on paper, make a real effort to try to solve or improve each item. You'll probably still have good reason to wear your T-shirt and say that thing you always say, but at least you'll be attempting to fix whatever it is that makes those words come out of your mouth.

- At the end of any given day, just after you've gotten home from work, find a quiet place in your home and record yourself simply talking about your day. Begin with the moment you got up, and then just talk about all the things that pop into your head as you think back on the day. Mention names, places, things that you saw on the way to work, what you got done, what you didn't get done, phone calls that you made and received, things that annoyed you, emails that you sent, overheard conversations, elevator banter, what you ate, the funny thing that happened on the way to that meeting. After you're done talking, hit stop, and replay the conversation for yourself. What message are you conveying to yourself about your current job?

WORKING FOR THE MAN
RULE #139 • A career coach's second book might be *How to Become a Career Coach*. The book won't do well, but the seminar based on the book, "Make $$$ as a Career Coach!" will bring in a little income.

THE ON-THE-CLOCK JOB HUNT

The best time to look for a new job is while you're on the clock, and not just to scour online job sites and draft cover letters. There are all kinds of resources to tap around the office, and the work environment itself is helpful—you should be running your job search just like you manage a work project, or rather, a work project that you care deeply about (as opposed to work projects that you despise, where you do everything and anything to avoid actually doing work on them, eventually turning in sub-par work and hoping no one notices what a bad job you did).

> **WORKING FOR THE MAN**
> **RULE #140** • A sign that it is time for you to find another job: When you are walking by the paper cutter, you think to yourself, *I should just stick my arm in there and bring down the slicer in one, swift, furious motion.*

- First, get your résumé updated. There's an art to putting a résumé together, a way of presenting all of your past and present job experience (and all the professional accomplishments implied) in a fantastical way. If you've been using the same résumé for years, just adding the most recent job on top of the last, then you are sorely in need of a thorough reworking of your résumé. Ask trusted coworkers to share with you how their résumés are worded, and get friends and colleagues to make comments on your new and improved résumé. You want it to shine and stand out. One option is to

WORKING FOR THE MAN
RULE #141 • Another sign that it is time to find another job: You think to yourself, regularly, *If I just run really fast and slam myself into the wall, by the time I wake up it will probably be five o'clock, and I can get the hell out of here.*

establish a secret résumé-writing workshop with those above mentioned trusted coworkers—the people you go out and get drinks with and say a little too much about how you really feel about so and so, your boss, or about the job in general. Get together on the clock or after work at a bar, and work together to critique and improve each other's résumés.

- There's nothing like friendly competition to provide an incentive for finding a new job. Challenge your coworkers to a winner-takes-all race—the first person to find a new job, offer letter in hand, wins a cash money pot—something substantial. Of course you only want to involve coworkers you trust, but try to get people you dislike involved in the deal. Sure, competition is a great incentive, but no one likes to lose to people they despise—getting those people involved is incentive on top of incentive. Even if you don't win the actual competition, you'll win on a personal level by truly engaging in the hunt and working hard to land a new job.

- Set aside time every day to check in on the relevant job sites, and email or call any head hunters as often as possible, within reason. This may cut into the time you spend catching up on the latest gossip or fashions or sports news or, better yet, whatever high-priority, red-flagged project is due at the overused, artificially urgent "EOD," but it's important that you make the time to find out about as many job opportunities as possible, and apply for them all. Finding a new job is all about percentages—the more jobs you apply for, the better chance you have of landing a new one.

- When you do see jobs that are worth applying for, draft a cover letter tailored to each specific job. This is, of course, a major pain in the ass. But doing such work on the clock makes drafting tailor-made cover letters a lot less painful.

- You should always be doing this, but it's especially important when you have a new job on your mind: seek out projects that are résumé builders, things that make the news (industry news is fine). In other words, get assigned to and work on projects that are so clearly impressive that they have no need for the usual fluff and puff when you highlight them on your résumé. Only peripherally involved? That's okay. Just like junior architects tell people they designed the building, you can take a larger slice of the credit on

> **WORKING FOR THE MAN**
> **RULE #142** • Yet another sign: Every time you take note of the view out of one of the office windows, ten stories up, you think to yourself, *If I just start running as fast as I can from right here, I bet I could hurl myself through the thick glass and just end it all right fucking now.*

your résumé. NOTE: Your newfound enthusiasm regarding work projects may actually be so noticeable that you end up inadvertently landing yourself a raise and a promotion and, though it may seem totally inconceivable, a reason to stay put for a while.

- Make calls to friends and colleagues to find out about possible job openings, and ask them about any contacts they might have at companies you are interested in or that you've applied for jobs at. Reach out to vendors (salespeople) as well— especially ones who have an interest in keeping you happy, no matter what company you might be working for. Vendors know tons of people, have lots of inside information, and understand the power of doing a solid. Doing all this during the day from your desk adds a professional flair to the call. And hey, even if you don't find out about any new jobs, you never know what information might come your way—a cool party happening later in the week, a date, some good gossip on your boss or a coworker. Additional bonus: these phone calls take time, and have a way of making the end of the work day come a little quicker.

- Take advantage of any industry events or conferences. Usually you try to avoid these, going so far as to actively lobby against having to attend them. But these events are all about networking, and there is no better opportunity to meet lots of new people and hear about the latest trends and hot new companies and products. You should do everything you can to get to as many of these events as possible. Of course, instead of networking your company's products and services, your main goal is to network yourself. Be bold and introduce yourself to the most important

> **WORKING FOR THE MAN**
> **RULE #143** • If you happen to decide to dress nicely on a particular day, for no reason other than to upscale your usual look, one of your coworkers will be sure to ask, right within earshot of your boss, "How was the job interview?"

people attending. You are talking up the most important thing you've ever touted: yourself. Even if solid job leads do not materialize, at least an unlimited number of free drinks will be available to you at the countless industry parties, held throughout the conference, at the end of each day.

Overall, apply for as many jobs as you can, and don't ever turn down an interview. Seek out every opportunity and see how you can improve your bottom line. It's how the company you work for operates, and it's a system worth emulating in your own professional life. Remember, the company you work for isn't looking out for your best interests. Only you can do that. So while you are at work and on the clock, get to work—as diligently and efficiently as possible—on finding that new job.

> **WORKING FOR THE MAN**
> **RULE #144** • The best day you'll ever have at whatever your current job is will be your last day on said job.

THE JOB OFFER

If your boss arrives at the office in a bad mood and yells at you for no reason, you are still expected to work hard and do good work. If you come to the office in a bad mood and yell at your boss, maybe because he yelled at you the day before, your boss could fire you. That's the nature of the power dynamic in the workplace. You work for your boss. Your boss does not work for you.

And let's remember that most bosses don't even need to be in a bad mood to yell at their employees.

Now, some people in the workforce—hot-shot computer engineers, successful CEOs, salespeople with a solid track record—get a constant stream of phone calls from head hunters offering opportunities galore. These people have a high-desirability factor built into their job situation. Their employers know the score and act accordingly. They offer stock options, a year-end bonus, a hefty expense account, extra vacation days, a four-day work week, and more, not to mention the fact that these employees can act like jackasses and letches or a combination of both, and the higher-ups will look the other way. And while there's no promise of being treated well by a supervisor, you can bet your bottom dollar that these sought-after types will be treated a million times better than your average worker bee by even the meanest of bosses.

WORKING FOR THE MAN
RULE #145 • The best moment you'll ever have at whatever your current job is will be the last time you shut your office door, and walk out of the building for the very last time.

But most of us aren't so lucky. The only calls we're getting are from our parents, who keep begging us to go to law school.

However, in order to tip the balance of power in your favor, and steal away a little of the authority that your boss holds over you, you need to start getting calls. That's right, you need to get some job offers. A few offers every couple of months.

This is not as impossible as it seems. It's quite easy, actually.

So you're not a computer engineer, nor have you ever been on the cover of *BusinessWeek*. That doesn't matter. All you have to do is be a diligent job seeker. Similar to the way politicians operate in constant campaign mode even after they've just been elected, you need to operate as if you are desperately unemployed and looking for a job even though you are gainfully employed. Since you don't actually need a job, you don't have to feel that pit-in-your-stomach, nobody-wants-me, I'm-such-a-loser, how-am-I-going-to-pay-my-bills anxiety that haunts the truly unemployed.

In order to get this operation in motion, you must become a résumé mill. Send out résumés to any job that remotely fits into your professional parameters. The more résumés you send, the more interviews you'll get, and the greater the number of interviews, the more job offers you'll receive. And the higher the number of job offers, the more valued you become as an employee.

There are several things to keep in mind while you are going on these interviews. You don't want to be open with your boss about your job hunting activities, but you definitely want to have him speculating that you might indeed be seeking another job.

You can do this by wearing an especially nice suit on the days that you have an interview. But do your best to schedule interviews so that you aren't having to take lots of time off of work.

Now, if your boss asks you directly if you are looking for a job, simply offer a non-denial denial: "Just working hard to work my way up the career ladder!" Do not ever be direct. You want to keep your boss wondering.

That is, until you've got an offer you shouldn't refuse. Now it's time to play your boss, and if you play him right, you'll possibly end up with more money and definitely some more respect. The power shift is subtle while you ever so slightly let on that you're looking for a new job. When you've got an actual offer, it's time to pull out all the stops and back your boss into a corner.

Keep in mind that you have to be the kind of employee that has created a space at the company that couldn't easily be filled if you were to leave. This means that if you always show up to work late, leave early, do poor work, and do not follow through on your responsibilities, this plan is not going to work. In fact, your boss will be overjoyed that you might be leaving the company on your own volition. (Companies don't like to fire employees, because it leads to potential lawsuits and possibly paying for unemployment benefits.) So make sure you not only do good work, but constantly carve out new responsibilities, create increasingly efficient systems for completing your tasks, and launch innovative initiatives. The more indispensable you are, the more your company will do to keep you from jumping ship.

Once you get an offer, get all the details down on paper.

Note the salary, vacation days, stock options, medical and dental plan, 401(k) plan, expense account, and all other pertinent details. Then write down the financial elements that make up your current job. Once this is completed, make an appointment to talk to your boss. Don't just pull him aside and say, "I want to talk to you about something." A formalized meeting with a set period of time will establish a level of seriousness to the situation. Your boss will know that you are truly considering the offer, but have not yet made up your mind. You are setting the stage to negotiate. This is the moment where you will find out how much you are worth to your boss.

A smart boss will play it cool, and will usually just tell you that he'll have to get back to you. He might act annoyed, and most surely he is, given that if you leave, he'll have to waste time and money finding and training someone to take your place, or he'll have to pay you more money to keep you around. So far so good. You want your boss annoyed.

Do you really want to take this job you've been offered? If yes, then the pressure is off. Before you leave that office, make some crazy demands and see what happens. Ask for an outrageous salary increase. Literally demand what it would take to keep you from leaving. The odds are that your company won't be able to meet your demands, and off you go to a better job anyway.

But what if you do not want the job you've been offered? Then you have to play your hand perfectly. The pressure is definitely on. You don't want to get cornered into a phony ultimatum of your own making. A good option here is to play the dishonest "honesty" card. This means that you explain to your boss that you "in all honesty" don't really want to take the job, but you have to seriously consider the issues of a higher salary and an improved benefits package. This way, if your boss holds firm and says no dice, you aren't backed into a corner. You can simply say that you're getting more professionally from your current job, and that in the long run it will be better to stay put. For now anyway. Make sure to get the "for now" part across.

Even though it may seem like you've failed, you have actually been quite successful. You've put your boss on notice. He now knows that you are desirable to the outside world, and that you are actively seeking opportunity. Even though he didn't match the details of the offer, you will see improvements in your work situation: better assignments, a more sincere demeanor, less outrage at your mistakes, a higher degree of respect.

Keep in mind that there is no loyalty in the workplace anymore. You might be laid off during a downsizing, or perhaps after a merger. You may love your doctor, but if a cheaper health care plan is found, say goodbye to your doctor and hello to a new card and thick doctor directory from your new health care provider. Your company is loyal to the bottom line. It will shed no tears for you. But it works both ways. Indeed, it must work both ways. You do not have to have any loyalty to your company. If a better offer comes along during the middle of a major project, give your two weeks and don't ever look back. And don't feel guilty. If your spouse loses his/her job, or if one of your parents or kids gets sick, you can bet that won't prevent you from getting the ax during a downsizing. Companies live by the numbers, and so should you when it comes to making decisions about employment and your career.

TWO WEEKS' NOTICE

You fantasize about sex, you wish you could win the lottery, you have a dream house, you reminisce about your white-sand, clear-blue-water vacation, but a daydream that you might be overlooking are the glorious two weeks after you give notice. All those long-range plans? Irrelevant. All those spreadsheets that need to be updated? Not by you. Can't get to the office on time? Stop and grab some breakfast on the way, and get in even later. Not quite five o'clock? Leave anyway.

This little slice of heaven is just a new job offer away. Winning the lottery, your dream house, that beach vacation, and even sex might be totally out of reach, but finding a new job is totally within the safe confines of the reasonable realm of possibility. So be prepared to take advantage of those two special weeks—the best you'll have at any job if you're smart about it. Write out—just as you would a carefully prepared report for your boss—exactly what you plan to do after you give notice.

This is the time to remember all the crap that you've put up with on the job, all the late nights you've been forced to work, the lousy salary you've been paid, the nightmarish tasks you've been assigned, the way your boss has yelled at you. Let it all come back and get fresh in your mind. Let the sparks of anger tingle up your spine, for every last moment of the two-week notice is your time to get a little something in return for all the work you've done and all the nonsense you've had to deal with, as well as a little payback:

The List. On that first day of the two-week countdown, sit at your desk and focus like you've never focused before on making a list of all the things you hate about your job. This list serves a number of purposes. First, it gives you concrete examples to focus on as you embark on your mission of payback. Two, it provides a list of all the things to avoid, such as meetings and deadlines, as well as specific people to shun, treat like shit, and take revenge on. Three, in case you start to feel an impulse of loyalty toward your company, and actually start to feel guilty about your new attitude of nonchalance, you can read over the list and be reminded of the horrible nature of your job.

Relax. Once the list is complete, it's time to slow down the pace. Sit back. Enjoy a cup of coffee. Hell, enjoy two or three. Buy some magazines and read them from cover to cover. Send email to friends. Surf the web. Make lots of long distance phone calls. Look into that trip to Mexico you've always meant to take. When you go on a break, make it a long one. Go run some errands. This is no longer company time. It's your time.

Take your sick days. If you've got sick days left, now is the time to use them. The key here is not to feel guilty, or even awkward, about calling in sick during your two-week-notice period. Even if you've got five sick days, take every last one of them. It's your time to squeeze something from the company in return for all your hard work, and taking your sick days is one of the ways to get compensation.

Show up late. The number of times you've felt panic swell up in your chest and sweat beads dampen your forehead in the dead of winter because you were late for work is too many to count. All that wasted energy! All the stress! All because your boss has sternly warned you that the workday starts at

8:30 a.m., and not 8:40 a.m. Well, during your last two weeks, the workday starts when you want it to. If you're late, and you get caught, just make up an excuse. And feel free to use the most basic of excuses: "My car wouldn't start" or "There was a power outage and my alarm clock didn't go off this morning." Don't worry about whether or not it raises an eyebrow. You know it's not worth the effort to think up a more elaborate rationale for your tardiness, and your boss knows that she's run out of runway in terms of busting your chops over your lack of discipline and subpar work ethic.

Take really, really long lunches. During these last two weeks, consider the start of the lunch break to be the very moment in which you feel hungry. So if your stomach growls at 10:30 a.m., go to lunch. And once you've gone to lunch, take your time. Look the menu over long and hard. Buy the paper and read every section. Meet up with an old friend on the other side of town. Order dessert and coffee. Do whatever it takes to make it seem more like Sunday brunch.

Steal office supplies and other things you've always wanted to take. Now, don't get greedy. Don't steal anything that will jeopardize your new job, or God forbid get you jail time, if you get caught. This is simply your time to stock up on office supplies, and maybe a few coffee cups. Raid that supply cabinet, and if you've got a special attachment to a stapler on your desk, slip it in your bag and take it home. You deserve it!

Sabotage your ongoing work. If you've got an ongoing assignment or something that you've been working on that you're not going to finish before your final exit, delete it, or jumble it up into a complete state of disarray. It's your work, after all. Why should the person who comes in after you've left get credit for something you've put together? More than likely, you will leave your supervisor in the lurch. That's icing on the cake. Lord knows he's never done anything to help you out, and has essentially made his life better by making yours more miserable.

Revenge. That list of things you hate about your job is sure to include a few coworkers and, as sure as the copy machine will be out of service the next time you need to use it, the name of your boss. Unless your coworkers are exceptionally annoying, let your revenge on them be the fact that you're leaving and they aren't. But your boss, he's the asshole who is principally behind all the crap you've had to put up with. He is the force that has created the swell of stress, unhappiness, and general discontent in the better part of your waking hours. He deserves to literally get thrown out of the main office doors, but that wouldn't be revenge—that would be playing right into the hand of "The Man." You'd lose your new job (with zero chance of collecting unemployment) and, most likely, go to jail. The last thing you want to hear is your boss saying, "Of course I want to press charges, Officer." So you are left to do the more innocuous, simple actions that will momentarily derail the flow of your boss's day. Throw out some of his messages. File some of his papers in the wrong cabinets. Yank some pages from the middle of an important document and throw them out. Lose some of his outgoing mail. Dump some of the incoming mail. Make sure he doesn't get the recently circulated memo. Hide his staple remover. Put a bunch of pens that don't work in his desk drawer. Sure, these things seem petty, but just remember the times he asked you, in front of a client, to go make copies of a document. Remember the times late on Friday afternoons that he dropped assignments in your lap that had to be done by Monday morning. The times he had you pick up his lunch on rainy afternoons. The times he forgot to tell you he didn't need that research done after all.

Every job book out there will tell you in big, bold letters, "Don't quit your current job until you've found a new one," the reason being that you are more desirable to prospective employers if you are currently employed. Also, you won't be strapped for cash and be suffering from the stresses of unemployment while you desperately try to find a job. That's good advice, but it's leaving out a key reason: the joys of liberation and sweet revenge during your two weeks' notice.

MEMO
an interview hypothetical

Interviewer: "Sell me this pen."
(pen handed from interviewer to interviewee)

Interviewee: "This is an extraordinary pen that makes writing, whether you are penning a letter to a friend or just paying bills, a truly remarkable experience. With barely any pressure to the paper at all, the pen dispenses a fine, consistent amount of ink, thereby helping to prevent strain in the hand for even the longest of writing sessions.

This pen will never leak, and therefore can be carried around without any threat of ink stains on clothing. The pen is handsomely designed, as you can see. It's versatile, and would be appropriate in the office or at home in that drawer where the address book is kept. And lastly, the price is right. So how about giving this pen a try."
(pen handed back to interviewer from interviewee)

What the interviewee, rightly, wishes he could say . . .

Interviewer: "Sell me this pen."

(pen handed from interviewer to interviewee)

Interviewee: "Well, this pen is just a regular old pen. I'm not quite sure why you would want to purchase this particular pen over other pens. There are a lot of pens to choose from in the world, and I'd just like to be honest and point out that since I've never used the pen, I can't recommend this one over the other pens available. But having been asked to do this extremely stupid little exercise, I can now honestly say that there is one particular reason for getting ahold of this pen. I'm speaking from experience now, so you can feel quite comfortable taking my word as truth. If you happen to be job hunting in the near future, and during job interviews you are asked stupid questions by an interviewer, perhaps asked to present a hypothetical sales pitch on something that you've never seen before and have no interest in whatsoever, you could uncap this pen, grip it like you're trying to stir through thick cookie dough, and use it to stab your interviewer right in the eye. A whole bunch of times, really quickly. The sharp point on this pen right here will maximize clean, swift entries and exits, and enhance the precision of the continuous blows. Why don't you lean forward and get a little closer so that you can get a real good look at the exquisitely sharp tip of this pen . . ."

(pen uncapped and not handed back to the interviewer)

MEMO
things that might be said in a job interview that should concern you gravely

- "We have a lot of fun around here."
- "We're like family here."
- "When my wife was in labor at the hospital, the boss let me leave a few minutes early so that I could be with her."
- "We work weekends all of the time, but the managers will order in pizza and let you turn on a radio quietly or listen to your iPod."
- "This is the kind of place where people take care of each other."
- "We're all team players here."
- "We try to reward our employees for all their hard work. Like last Friday morning, we brought each and every employee a muffin and orange juice right to their desk."
- "The work can get difficult, but we all really enjoy the challenge."
- "This company brings out the best in people."
- "We provide our employees with the kind of experience that's worth way more than their salary."
- "Keeping up worker morale is a top priority at our company. That's why we recently instituted a 'Casual Friday' program."
- "Management works hard to keep in touch with the employees. There is a management meeting every week

just to go over notes that employees have placed in the
suggestion box."

- "It's usually so crazy here that I forget to go home."
- "We really reward worker enthusiasm here. For example, we give a $100 bonus to the employee that wears
that best costume to work on Halloween every year."

THE THANK-YOU NOTE: WHAT YOU HAVE TO WRITE / WHAT YOU WISH YOU COULD WRITE

The Basic Interview Thank-You Note:

Dear Sylvia,

Thank you very much for the opportunity to interview for
a position in the finance department. I enjoyed meeting
you and learning more about the company. I'm very interested in the position, and I hope to hear from you soon.

Best regards,

Iam Brown-Knowser

The Honest, If Only I Didn't Have to Get Down on My Hands and Knees and Kiss Your Ass Thank-You Note:

Sylvia,

I wish I could say thanks, but I really don't have anything to be grateful for, given the horrible nature of the

way you conducted my recent job interview. In short, you are a moron.

First of all, you didn't have a copy of my résumé on hand. I had to supply you with a copy. Perhaps this was some silly little test, to see if I was prepared enough for the interview, extra copies dutifully available like a good little interviewee. But you aren't the busy director of finance. It's your job to be prepared to interview me. Having my résumé on hand would have been a good place to start. Get your act together, Sylvia.

Second, you didn't remember a thing from our fifteen-minute telephone conversation three days before the interview. Didn't you take any notes? I had to keep correcting you on important details, like the fact that I am currently employed, not out of work, and repeating answers to your lame questions, questions I had already addressed in our earlier conversation. Get with the program, Sylvia. Stop wasting my time. Not your time. My time.

Third, your basic, run-of-the-mill questions are only going to get you the basic, boilerplate answers. How many times are we, *those who are looking for jobs,* going to be subjected to questions like "Tell me about a time that you were professionally successful?" You are boring us, Sylvia. It's like someone plugged you in and hit the start button on a program that loops inane, pointless banter. Mix it up a little. Get creative. Stop being such a status-quo human resources drone.

Fourth, if you open up the interview for questions, please, PLEASE, be sure that you can answer the questions posed to you. I know you wanted something simple, like "What are the people like who work here?" or "What is the dress code?" but I'm not going to give up my current job unless I know some solid information about the company you are doing the hiring for, questions about new products, systems, management, the current state of the marketplace, and emerging competitors. Clearly, you had no idea. And your lame attempts at answering the questions only made you seem even more pathetic. Please, take some time to learn about how your company works beyond the great seminars on retirement planning and casual dress code. Don't make your job solely about poring over résumés and conducting generic, lame interviews. If you try, you will most likely be able to break through your shell of ineptitude. Not that I'd put any money on that bet.

I'm sure this note has ruined my chances for a second interview. Good. Any company that allows you to be the gatekeeper on who is hired and who is not hired is surely doomed to failure.

—T. Ruth Betold

WRITE YOUR OWN RULES

Working for the Man Rule #146 is that there is no end to the number of Working for the Man Rules. You know best how it works around your office. Write down your own

> **WORKING FOR THE MAN RULE #146** • There is no end to the number of Working for the Man Rules.

rules, and then distribute throughout the office, maybe even post them on that bulletin board they hung up in the bathroom so no one would deface the stalls—just doing your honor-bound duty to enforce the laws of cubicle land.

REMEMBER WORKING FOR THE MAN RULE #1: We are all working for the man.

ABOUT THE AUTHOR

Jeffrey Yamaguchi threw himself a retirement party at the age of twenty-six. No, he had not won the lottery or benefited from a stock options windfall. It was just wishful thinking, which continues on to this day. More of his schemes can be found at www.workingfortheman.com and www.52projects.com.

ABOUT THE ILLUSTRATOR

Danny Jock, an artist in Brooklyn, has done thousands of drawings from life. His work can be seen at www.medium rarepub.com.